THE FREEDOM PRINCIPLE

THE FREEDOM
PRINCIPLE

LANSING POLLOCK

Prometheus Books

BUFFALO, NEW YORK 14215

Published 1981 by Prometheus Books
700 East Amherst Street, Buffalo, New York 14215

Library of Congress Catalog Card Number: 81-81709
ISBN 0-87975-157-6
Printed in the United States of America

To My Parents

CONTENTS

Preface

The idea that there is something morally wrong with using or manipulating other persons to further one's own ends has held an attraction for many philosophers. It is often assumed that when we use others "as a mere means" we do not show proper respect for their dignity. Consider the example of the student who cheats on an examination. The particular act of cheating may have good or bad consequences, but in either case, the consequences do not seem relevant to whether the cheater has acted immorally. The cheater has used the instructor to further his own ends; successful cheating requires deception, and the instructor is the victim of that deception.[1] What is wrong with this? The cheater treats the instructor as if he were a tool that the cheater can use for his own purposes. What he disregards is the fact that the instructor is also a person who has his own values, purposes, and goals. Because he is a person, the instructor has a dignity that other persons should respect, and to cause him to behave involuntarily by using deception does not show proper respect for his dignity as a self-directing agent.

It will be my contention that the freedom principle captures the intuitive idea that we should not use other persons (without their consent) to further our own ends. According to the freedom principle, each person ought to grant other persons an equal right to be free. As a general rule, a person violates this principle when he tries to impose his values upon others. Thus, in most cases, a person should not use force or threats to coerce others into doing what he wants, and he should not employ deception to cause others to act contrary to their own values. The freedom principle has important implications for political philosophy, for it entails severe moral restrictions on what government can rightfully do. Those who believe that "big brother" plays too large a role in our lives will be pleased with this conclusion. Those who believe in the "supportive state" obviously will not be. However, I shall argue that a free society, a society based on the freedom principle, has many attractive qualities. Indeed, I claim that it is utopia, i.e., the best possible society.

The views expressed in this book can be classified as libertarian. The roots of libertarian thought go back to the "natural rights" tradition of the seventeenth century. According to this tradition, persons have rights that are not conferred by governments, and governments should protect (and not violate) these rights. John Locke stated that "the law of nature stands as an eternal rule to all men, legislators as well as others."[2] Thus, Locke held that the law of nature provides a criterion for judging the positive laws enacted by the state. In particular, all men are entitled to enjoyment of the rights to life, liberty, and estate, and governments that violate these rights are illegitimate.

> Whenever the legislators endeavor to take away and destroy the property of the people, or to reduce them to slavery under arbitrary power, they put themselves into a state of war with the people who are thereupon absolved from any further obedience.... What I have said here concerning the legislative in general holds true concerning the supreme executor, who having a double trust in him—both to have a part in the legislative and the supreme execution of the law—acts against both when he goes about to set up his own arbitrary will as the law of the society.[3]

The influence of Locke on eighteenth century American thought can be seen in the Declaration of Independence. Thomas Jefferson wrote that all men have equal rights to life, liberty, and the pursuit of happiness and that governments are instituted in order to protect these rights. The founding fathers, having experienced British tyranny, feared a concentration of power in the hands of the federal government. They therefore established a limited government with carefully circumscribed powers. There was no direct taxation of income; the federal government acquired its revenue primarily from import duties. The federal government did not engage in public works like building roads or canals. The federal government was not involved in education, and there were no welfare programs to help the poor. There was very little regulation of commerce and industry. In short, it was a government that satisfied Thoreau's maxim: "That government is best which governs least."[4]

Contemporary America has obviously strayed from its libertarian foundations. Some would argue that changes were necessitated by the complexities of modern society. However, others claim that big government is often the cause of our problems. Dissatisfaction with big government has led to the growth of a new libertarian movement in the United States. In recent years, a consensus within this movement has developed on a number of key issues. For example, libertarians favor a noninterventionist foreign policy; they oppose military conscription, "victimless crime" laws, interference with voluntary economic exchanges, and compulsory participation in the social security system. The reader should note that libertarians do not fit comfortably on the left-right political spectrum. The Libertarian Party has often been classified as being right-wing. However, libertarian views on foreign policy and personal liberties are very different from typical right-wing views. Libertarians, unlike contemporary conservatives, are consistent advocates of limited government.

I should warn the reader that I will be developing a moral *theory*. As a result, the ideas presented in the first chapter, for example, will be developed throughout the course of the book. When particular parts are considered in isolation, the treatment of an issue may appear superficial. However, since the various parts are interrelated, they can only be judged in relation to the rest of the book. What is said in Chapter 1 anticipates what will be said in Chapter 7, and what is said in Chapter 7 depends on what was said in the previous chapters.

I have received aid and encouragement from many persons. I owe a particular debt of gratitude to my former teachers, Alan Gewirth and Warner Wick. My colleagues James Grunebaum, George Hole, and John Carbonara have helped me with their encouragement and their criticisms. I have learned much from the writings of and from correspondence with Lawrence Becker, Alan Donagan, Tibor Machan, and Marcus Singer. My friends John Jacobi, Michael Stansbury, and Peter Hogue provided valuable criticisms of earlier versions of the manuscript. I must also thank Steven Mitchell and Marilyn Coyne for their help in preparing the final version. Some of my other debts, too numerous to mention here, are acknowledged in the text.

Chapter One

The Freedom Principle

1.1 According to the freedom principle, each person ought to grant other persons an equal right to be free. The freedom principle requires reciprocal respect for autonomy. I (for example) should respect the autonomy of other persons, and other persons should respect my autonomy. Thus, interactions between myself and others should be based on mutual consent. In this case, the equal right of each person to be self-directing is respected.

The freedom principle applies to persons. Let us stipulate that a person is a human being who has the capacity (actual or potential) to act autonomously. The behavior of an autonomous agent is not determined by instinctive responses to immediate stimuli. Instead, the autonomous agent has a conception of time which allows him to understand the relationship between past and present circumstances, and he can anticipate future happenings. He also has conceptions of value that he can use in deciding what is worth doing. He can make judgments about the worth of different ends and the appropriateness of various means. In short, a

13

person is autonomous in the sense in which he is able to take a long-range point of view and act according to conceptions of value that he has adopted.[1]

Let us now connect what has been said about autonomy with the idea of giving meaning to one's life. I assume that a person gives meaning to his life by choosing to pursue ends that he values. "Giving meaning to one's life" combines two notions: purpose and value. What one is doing has a point in terms of one's aims and goals, and one believes that his aims and goals are worth pursuing. In an important sense, a person defines himself in terms of the aims and goals that he chooses to pursue; a person tells others who he is when he describes his most important ends.

To respect the autonomy of others, we must grant them an equal right to give meaning to their lives. In other words, each person should be granted an equal right to determine for himself what his own good is and how to pursue it. Due to different circumstances, abilities, and interests, aims and objectives will vary with each individual. If we wish to respect the autonomy of each person, we must accept this diversity. So long as persons do not violate the equal right of others to be free, we must allow them to be different.

1.2 Respect for autonomy is an idea that usually finds a sympathetic audience in Western democracies. However, it remains to be determined just what this idea entails. We respect a person's autonomy when we grant him the equal right to seek his own good in his own way. In contrast, we do not respect a person's autonomy (in most cases) when we cause the person to behave involuntarily.[2] Let us now examine (in general terms) the different ways in which a person can cause another person to behave involuntarily. First, A can cause B to behave involuntarily by using force. When A restrains B by knocking him down, tying him up, and throwing him in a cell, A has obviously caused B to behave involuntarily. Going beyond such obvious cases, I am using 'force' in the broad sense that includes taking or damaging something that belongs to another person. The thief, for example, who takes my car may not forcibly restrain me because I am not present when the theft occurs. Still, this would be a case in which force is used. The rationale for this will be considered in the chapter on property, (4.2).

A can also cause B to behave involuntarily by using a threat. I shall assume that a threat (by definition) always involves the threat of the use of force against the person who is threatened or against someone or something that he cares about. A threat renders a person's behavior involuntary when the person does something that he would not have chosen to do had no threat been made. What is the difference between a threat and an offer? When B refuses an offer from A, he has no reason to believe that A will use force to make him worse off. If A threatens B, then A gives B reason to believe that A will make him worse off if he refuses to do what A demands. Threats should also be distinguished from refusals to cooperate. For example, suppose that Sue tells Joe that she will not marry him unless he gets a steady job. Obviously, Sue has not threatened to use force against Joe. She has simply stated the conditions under which she will agree to get married.

Finally, let us note that A can cause B to behave involuntarily by deceiving B. In this kind of case, B's behavior would be involuntary due to ignorance. For example, suppose that B works for A because A has promised to pay B for his labor, when in fact, A does not intend to pay B. B's behavior would be involuntary since he would not have chosen to work for A if he had known that A would not pay him. Deception need not be intentional.[3] If B acts on the basis of misinformation supplied by A, A still would have caused B to behave involuntarily even if A did not intend to deceive B (e.g., A thought that his information was accurate).

In light of our examination of autonomy, let us say that a person is free to the extent that he is able to pursue his ends without interference from other persons.[4] Let us also stipulate that A interferes with B when A causes B to behave involuntarily. As a general rule, the freedom principle requires noninterference. Thus, in most cases where A causes B to behave involuntarily by using force, threat, or deception, A does not grant B an equal right to be free.

While the freedom principle requires noninterference in most cases, there are some exceptions to this rule. These are *not* exceptions to the freedom principle itself; instead, they involve cases in which interference does not violate the principle. I argue in Chapter 2, for example, that paternalistic acts do not violate the principle when the interference causes a person to behave in accordance with his *own* values. There are also cases in which self-defense and punishment do not violate the freedom principle. The principle entails that persons have a basic right—the equal right to be free. I argue in Chapter 3 that persons can defend their basic right without violating the freedom principle.

To summarize, there are cases in which self-defense, punishment, and paternalism do not violate the freedom principle. However, when none of the exceptions to the noninterference rule apply, a person violates the principle when he causes another person to behave involuntarily.

1.3 What does the word 'cause' mean in the phrase 'cause another person to behave involuntarily'? There is, I believe, nothing unusual about this use of the word. The word is of course ambiguous, but this usually creates no problem.[5] For example, in the statement "The fire was caused by the discarded cigarette," the discarded cigarette is neither a necessary nor a sufficient condition for starting the fire. It is not a necessary condition because other things could have started the fire, and it is not a sufficient condition because other things (oxygen and combustible material) must be present for the fire to start. Given that several factors are jointly sufficient for the fire to start, why do we pick out the discarded cigarette and call it "the cause"? We call the discarded cigarette the cause because it is unusual in the sense that it changes the status quo. Likewise, a threat may be neither a necessary nor a sufficient condition for B to do x. However, we can still say that the threat caused B to do x because it was the unusual event that changed the status quo. And even though other factors might have caused B to do x, from the moral point of view it is important to note that, assuming that other relevant factors did not change, B would not have chosen to do x had no prior threat been made. For example, B would not have given his wallet to the gunman had he not been threatened.

When we say "Colds are caused by viruses," we are pointing to a necessary condition as the cause. Contact with a cold virus is not a sufficient condition for catching a cold; other conditions such as low resistance are necessary as well. Likewise, when we say "B's behavior was caused by A's deception," we may mean that the deception was a necessary, but not a sufficient, condition for B's behavior. In other words, B would not have done x had he not been deceived, but other factors such as particular aspects of B's personality also influenced his behavior.

When we say "Smith's death was caused by heart failure," we have found a cause that is a sufficient condition for the occurrence of the event. Likewise, there will be cases in which the use of force will be a sufficient condition for the occurrence of a person's bodily movements. When B is tied up, carried to a prison, and thrown in a cell, the force used is a sufficient condition for B's behavior.[6] Some readers may feel an inclination to restrict the use of the word 'cause' to cases in which we know the sufficient conditions for the occurrence of the events. However, such a restriction is not consistent with ordinary usage, and I see no compelling reason to adopt it.

1.4 Suppose that Joe asks Sue to marry him and Sue refuses his proposal. It should be clear that Sue has not violated the freedom principle. She has not caused Joe to behave involuntarily by using force, threat, or deception. It is simply her unwillingness to do what Joe wants that thwarts his objective. Sue ought to grant Joe an *equal* right to be free, not an absolute right to be free. The equal right of Sue and Joe to be free is respected when they can reach a mutual and voluntary agreement on how to interact. If they cannot reach such an agreement, then there is no basis for an interaction which will respect the equal right of both to be free.

Suppose that Joe asks Bill for money, and Bill refuses to comply with the request. Once again, this example illustrates the important difference between non-cooperation and interference. Bill has not caused Joe to behave involuntarily; instead, they have simply failed to reach agreement on how to interact. This example illustrates one of the radical implications of the freedom principle. As a general rule, we are not morally required to help others. I am assuming that a person has a moral requirement only if we can justifiably compel the person to behave in accordance with the requirement. For example, if Bill is morally required to help Joe, then we have the right to compel Bill to help. We could, for example, tax Bill and use the money to help Joe. However, notice that, if we tax Bill in this case, our action would conflict with his right to noninterference. We would be causing Bill to behave involuntarily in a situation where none of the exceptions to the noninterference rule (i.e., self-defense, punishment, or paternalism) apply. Paternalism is irrelevant because we would be taxing Bill, not for his own good, but in order to help Joe. Self-defense and punishment do not apply because Bill does not cause Joe to behave involuntarily when he refuses to cooperate. Thus, we must conclude that Bill is not morally required to help Joe, and when this conclusion is generalized, we see that government welfare programs financed by coercive taxes are immoral, (see 4.4).

There are two exceptions to the general rule which states that we are not morally required to help others. First, we may have a duty to help others because of agreements we have made. For example, suppose that Smith and Jones decide to undertake a risky business venture. To get Jones's cooperation, Smith signs a legal agreement stating that he will provide Jones with financial assistance if the business fails. Let us suppose that the business does fail and Smith refuses to carry out the terms of the agreement. In this case, Jones would be morally justified in seeking a court order that would compel Smith to pay. If Smith refuses to honor their agreement, he violates the freedom principle by causing Jones to act involuntarily due to ignorance. Jones would not have chosen to participate in the risky business venture if he had not been assured that Smith would provide financial assistance if the business failed.

The second category of exceptions pertains to the parental duty to care for one's offspring. Since parents are responsible for producing a person who cannot see to his own needs, they have a duty to care for their child until he is able to care for himself. The basis for this duty can be seen by considering an analogous case. Suppose that you lock a person in a cell without food or water. If the person dies, you have killed him, because you are responsible for producing his helpless condition. Likewise, parents are responsible for producing a helpless child, and so they are held responsible for killing the child if it dies due to their neglect. And since killing is (usually) wrong according to the freedom principle, the principle entails that parents have a duty to care for their children. I shall say more about this duty in Chapter 2.

Many persons believe that our duty to help others goes beyond the limited view expressed above. However, I should emphasize that I am using 'duty' in the strong sense in which duties entail correlative rights. If you have a duty to help Jones, then Jones can demand your help *as his right*. Obviously you cannot have a duty to help everyone who is in need because you cannot have a duty to do the impossible. Furthermore, we can hold that helping others is good without holding that we have a duty to do it, (see 7.1). And those who enforce a broader notion of the duty to help violate the freedom principle. They impose their values on others, and thus they deny others an equal right to determine for themselves what their own good is and how to pursue it.

1.5 Is the freedom principle an egalitarian moral principle? In one obvious respect it is, for it requires that all persons be granted an *equal* right to be free. However, there are numerous inequalities that are consistent with the freedom principle. For example, as we shall see in Chapter 4, the principle allows for inequalities in wealth. What should we say then about the claims that the principle is or is not an egalitarian moral principle?

'Equality' is the name of a relation, the relation of sameness or identity.[7] For example, if several objects are equal in weight, they have the same weight. If two things are equal in value, they have the same value, etc. When a person tells us that equality is an important moral value, we should not take his comment literally. In other words, we should not assume that he values the relation of sameness or identity. Instead, he probably favors certain equalities and opposes certain inequalities. Hence, the first rule in discussions about equality should be to specify the kind of equality (or equalities) that one favors. We find out what the person who advocates equality really values when he tells us *what* it is that he thinks should be equal.

It is a fact that human beings differ in respect to characteristics like physical attractiveness, strength, talent, intelligence, drive, perseverance, etc. As a result, every demand for making human beings equal in some respect entails treating them unequally in other respects. For example, if we wish to make a group of people equal in athletic ability, we would have to handicap those with superior talent, or we would have to provide special training for the mediocre that would not be given to those who are naturally gifted. If we wish to equalize wealth, we will have to restrict the activities of those who have a special talent for making money. When persons with unequal talent participate in voluntary economic exchanges, unequal accumulations of wealth will result. Hence, to equalize wealth, we would have to place restrictions on the economic freedom of the talented. The general result of this analysis is that we see once again that "the egalitarian" cannot simply favor equality. He must tell us *what* it is that he thinks should be equal.

The person who claims to be an egalitarian may be claiming that persons should be granted equal initial rights. For example, he may think that citizens should be granted equal political rights such as the right to vote, the right to run for office, and the right to express political beliefs. However, once again we must note that, since human beings differ, such equal initial rights will result in unequal political power. For example, those who have a special talent for articulating their political beliefs can make more effective use of their right to express their political opinions.

Some advocates of equality seem to hold that equality of opportunity is an absolute moral value. If we stipulate that equality of opportunity means providing everyone with an equal start in life, then this is a very radical position. To give everyone an equal (i.e., the same) start in life, we would have to take children away from their parents in order to try to insure that all children are raised in the same environment. And those who had the responsibility of shaping this early environment would have more power than other persons (i.e., unequal power).

Is the freedom principle an egalitarian moral principle? It is as egalitarian as any other moral principle. As a proponent of the freedom principle, I favor certain equalities and oppose certain inequalities. And that is all that any "advocate of equality" can do.

1.6 I shall conclude this chapter with an examination of how the freedom principle differs from some other moral principles to which it bears a superficial resemblance. Consider, for example, the following principle—All persons have the right to be free so long as they do not infringe upon the like liberty of others. This principle has two components: the first is positive in that it states that persons have the right to be free, while the second states what the limits of this right are. However, the principle is ambiguous, for its second component is subject to different interpretations.[8]

According to what I shall call the specific interpretation, a person has the right to do any act so long as he leaves others free to do the same kind of act. For example, A would have the right to assault B so long as he did not injure B to the extent that B would be unable to do the same kind of act (i.e., assault A or someone else). By similar reasoning, A could claim the right to lie, steal, cheat, etc. In contrast, such acts are prohibited by the freedom principle (in most cases) because they violate the noninterference rule. In particular cases, the exceptions to the noninterference rule (self-defense, punishment, and paternalism) might apply. However, whether the agent leaves his victim free to do the same kind of act is not relevant to determining if the noninterference rule has been violated.

According to what I shall call the general interpretation of the principle, a person has the right to be free so long as he does not prevent others from doing what they want to do. Let us first note that, on this interpretation, the principle differs from the freedom principle because it rules out all paternalistic acts. The *only* ground for interfering with a person is that he is preventing *others* from doing what they want to do. Secondly, let us consider what the principle entails in the following case. A and B are attending an auction, and they both want the same painting. According to the general interpretation of the principle, A does not have the right to outbid B because this would prevent B from doing what he wants to do. Likewise, B would not have the right to outbid A because this would prevent A from doing what he wants to do. In general, this principle often requires inaction when the desires of different persons conflict. In contrast, A does not violate the freedom principle when he outbids B because he does not interfere with B, i.e., he does not cause B to behave involuntarily by using force, threat, or deception.

In *On Liberty,* Mill introduces a principle that might be confused with the freedom principle. Mill claims that he has "one very simple principle" that will tell us when we have the right to be free.

...the only purpose for which power can be rightfully exercised over any member of a civilized community, against his will, is to prevent harm to others. His own good, either physical or moral, is not a sufficient warrant.[9]

I understand Mill to be saying that "to prevent harm to others" is a necessary condition (but not a sufficient condition) for justified interference. Thus, the principle does not tell us when interference is justified; instead, it tells us when we should *not* interfere. If interference does not prevent harm to *others,* it is unjustified. Mill's principle differs from the freedom principle by ruling out all paternalistic acts.[10]

Other differences will depend on how the key word 'harm' is interpreted. In the first chapter, Mill gives the impression that he is going to use the notion of harm to help us identify what some of our rights are. In the fourth chapter, Mill tells us that often we must know what rights persons have in order to know whether they have been harmed.

The acts of an individual may be hurtful to others, or wanting in due consideration for their welfare, without going the length of violating any of their constituted rights. The offender may then be justly punished by opinion, though not by law.[11]

The distinction between the loss of consideration which a person may rightly incur by defect of prudence or of personal dignity, and the reprobation which is due him for an offense against the rights of others, is not a merely nominal distinction. It makes a vast difference both in our feelings and in our conduct toward him, whether he displeases us in things in which we think we have a right to control him, or in things in which we know that we have not.[12]

It would appear that Mill has led us in a circle. We must understand the notion of harm in order to determine what rights persons have, but we must already know what rights persons have in order to know whether they have been harmed. Mill can escape from this circle by providing us with an independent moral theory that will tell us what our rights are. Mill does have a moral theory; he is a utilitarian.

> It is proper to state that I forego any advantage which could be derived to my argument from the idea of abstract right, as a thing independent of utility. I regard utility as the ultimate appeal on all ethical questions; but it must be utility in the largest sense, grounded on the permanent interests of man as a progressive being.[13]

Utilitarians tell us to maximize the good. The basic value in Mill's utilitarian theory is happiness, and thus Mill recommends that we act in ways that produce the most happiness. Furthermore, he holds that we will maximize happiness if we follow his liberty principle which is "entitled to govern absolutely the dealings of society with the individual in the way of compulsion and control."[14] But how can Mill know this? Even if we become clear about what happiness is (and Mill was never clear about this), how can we know that following Mill's liberty principle will produce the most happiness *in every case?* For example, how can Mill know that refraining from paternalistic acts will always result in the greatest happiness? What is worse is that we probably cannot determine what will produce the most happiness *in any* (particular) *case.* Since we lack the proverbial crystal ball that would allow us to see the future, it is hard to know what to make of a moral theory that asks us to act on knowledge that we do not have. As Alan Donagan notes, "what ought to astonish readers of their work is neither the complexity nor the difficulty of utilitarian calculations, but their absence."[15] Until a utilitarian shows us that he can do *one* utilitarian calculation dealing with a fairly complex case, it is hard to take the utilitarian theory seriously.

One problem that utilitarians must resolve concerns the number of alternatives that a person must examine when he does a utilitarian calculation. The number of things that a normal person in normal circumstances can do at any given moment seems to be limited only by his imagination. For example, I am not thinking seriously about leaving my wife and children, but perhaps this act combined with others would have the highest utility. Perhaps I should go to South America and help the poor. How can I know unless I do the requisite utilitarian calculation? How many alternatives should I be examining right now? Am I doing the act that has the highest utility?

Another question that utilitarians must resolve is whether the general use of the utility principle would have the highest utility. Perhaps persons should be taught a set of "simple" rules which they should follow instead of trying to calculate the utility of their acts in each case. However, this approach becomes complicated because rules will conflict; hence, utilitarian calculations may still be necessary in order to settle conflicts between rules. How many rules would a set of "simple" rules have? The possibility for conflicts increases as more rules are added. On the other hand, if the set contains only a few rules, they will probably be inadequate to cover many moral situations—unless the rules are very general (like the golden rule). But if the rules are very general, they will require interpretation which will increase the likelihood that they will be misapplied. Readers of *On Liberty,* for example, know that applications of the liberty principle can be quite complicated.

A third problem concerns the failure of utilitarians to produce an adequate theory of value. Utilitarians tell us to maximize the good, but what is the good that we are supposed to maximize? To see the magnitude of this problem, consider the following list of things that might be said to have intrinsic value: pleasure, the avoidance of pain, happiness, self-preservation, friendship, love, familial bonds, security, social cooperation, success, religious faith, keeping one's commitments, compassionate acts, generous acts, personal freedom, self-respect, self-perfection, self-realization, knowledge, and artistic excellence. This list is not complete, but it does illustrate the utilitarian's problem. If different things have intrinsic value, pursuit of these things can lead to conflicts. For example, the person who seeks knowledge may have to sacrifice security; the person who wants to be successful may have to give up many of his hedonistic pursuits; the person who keeps his commitments may have to make sacrifices with respect to the pursuit of artistic excellence, etc. When there are conflicts, how can we determine which course of action will maximize the good?

This difficulty has motivated utilitarians to search for a "dominant end" that can be used to judge the relative worth of different goods.[16] This search has often led to the acceptance of hedonism. Bentham is a prime example:

Nature has placed mankind under the governance of two sovereign masters, *pain* and *pleasure*. It is for them alone to point out what we ought to do, as well as to determine what we shall do. On the one hand the standard of right and wrong, on the other the chain of causes and effects, are fastened to their throne. They govern us in all we do, in all we say, in all we think: every effort we can make to throw off our subjection, will serve but to demonstrate and confirm it.[17]

One thing to note is that Bentham does not offer us one dominant end. He offers us two distinct ultimate ends: the pursuit of pleasure and the avoidance of pain. Which of these ends is more important? Football players and boxers, for example, are willing to accept a great deal of physical and emotional pain. Why? Does the pleasure outweigh the pain? How do we "weigh" pleasures and pains? Even if we limit our concerns to the pursuit of pleasure, how do we know which pleasures to prefer? Is the pleasure of sex, for example, to be preferred to pleasures derived from helping other persons? As Rawls notes:

And then too there is the fact that there are different sorts of agreeable feelings themselves incomparable, as well as the quantitative dimensions of pleasure, intensity and duration. How are we to balance these when they conflict? Are we to choose a brief but intense pleasant experience of one kind of feeling over a less intense but longer pleasant experience of another? Aristotle says that the good man if necessary lays down his life for his friends, since he prefers a short period of intense pleasure to a long one of mild enjoyment, a twelvemonth of noble life to many years of humdrum existence. But how does he decide this? Further, as Santayana observes, we must settle the relative worth of pleasure and pain. When Petrarch says that a thousand pleasures are not worth one pain, he adopts a standard for comparing them that is more basic than either. The person himself must make this decision, taking into account the full range of his inclinations and desires, present and future. Clearly we have made no advance beyond deliberative rationality. The problem of a plurality of ends arises all over again within the class of subjective feelings.[18]

One of the complications that hedonists ignore is that many of our pleasures are complex, and thus it is not so easy to put other values in their proper (hedonistic) place. A complex pleasure is a good feeling in which other values play a determinate role. In other words, whether we feel good (or bad) depends on judgments based on other values that we hold to be important. Consider, for example, the pleasure (or pain) that Smith receives from seeing a ballet. Let us assume that Smith, who has had an interest in ballet for many years, has fairly definite beliefs about what is good choreography and dance technique. These values play a determinate role in how he feels about a performance. If he judges that the choreography and dance technique is good, he will enjoy the performance. If not, it will be an unpleasant experience.

Moral feelings are typically complex. I feel bad when I see an injustice; I feel good when I see the injustice corrected. I will not have the same feelings if my beliefs about justice change. For example, if I believe that preferential hiring programs are good because they correct past injustices, then I will feel good when I see these programs established. However, if I change my beliefs so that I hold that preferential hiring programs are themselves unjust, then I will feel bad when I see these programs established. In this case, and many others involving complex feelings, it is our values that determine whether we have good or bad feelings. And when our values determine whether we feel good or bad, it is obvious that pleasure cannot be used as the standard for judging which values are "more valuable."

I am not trying to substitute one oversimplification for another. I am not claiming that all feelings are complex. When I see a sunset, I am simply struck by the beauty of it. It is a pleasant experience, and since I have no beliefs about what makes a sunset beautiful, other values play no role in my good feelings. Thus, there are "simple" feelings as well as complex feelings. But complex feelings are quite common, and their existence plagues the hedonist. The hedonist wants good feelings to serve as his "raw data" that he can use in judging the value of other things. But in many cases, it is our values that determine whether our experiences are pleasant or unpleasant.

The difficulties encountered by the pleasure-pain theory of value have led some utilitarians to state their theories in terms of desires and satisfactions. According to this view, satisfaction of desire is the basic good. Unfortunately, when we scratch the surface of this theory of value, we find the same problems that plague the pleasure-pain theory. For example, if satisfying desires is good, then (presumably) dissatisfaction is bad. Thus the theory contains two ultimate ends (produce satisfaction and avoid dissatisfaction), and once again the utilitarian faces the problem of trying to weigh incommensurable values. Suppose that we must choose between two acts: act x will make A and B mildly satisfied while making C very dissatisfied, and act z will make A and B mildly dissatisfied while making C very satisfied. How can we weigh the satisfactions and dissatisfactions and determine which act will produce the most satisfaction? Suppose that C's dissatisfaction (if act x is chosen) would be due to a loss of self-respect, while A and B would experience physical pleasure. Surely these feelings are incommensurable, and thus we cannot determine whether act x produces more (or less) satisfaction than dissatisfaction.

Finally, we should note that this theory of value entails that the satisfaction of a person's desires is good *whatever* the person's desires may be. For example, satisfaction of the desires of the rapist, the robber, and the murderer is good according to this theory. The utilitarian can respond that it is our duty to maximize satisfactions. Hence, if the majority prefer not to be raped, robbed, or murdered, we can work to frustrate the desires of these persons. However, there is still the problem that what the majority wants may not be good. The majority, for example, may want to enslave a minority group. (Contemporary support for the military draft is a good example of this.) Human beings are not infallible, and what they desire is not a reliable indication of what is good. I conclude that utilitarians have yet to develop a plausible theory of value.

This examination of utilitarianism was prompted by Mill's insistence that his liberty principle is based on the utility principle. We (supposedly) maximize utility by following the liberty principle. However, since no one has developed an adequate utilitarian theory, there is no way to prove (or disprove) Mill's contention.

Chapter Two

Paternalism

2.1 As a general rule, the freedom principle requires noninterference. However, there are paternalistic acts that do not violate the principle. A paternalistic act is one in which concern for the welfare of another person is the primary reason for interfering with that person. In other words, paternalism is interfering with a person for that person's *own* good. Paternalistic acts do not violate the freedom principle when the interference causes the person to behave in accordance with his own values. In this kind of case, the agent is not denying the recipient an equal right to pursue his own good; instead the agent is helping the latter to behave in accordance with his own values.

Let us consider some simple cases which illustrate the above remarks. A person is standing under a falling rock, and you push him out of the way. You interfere (i.e., cause him to behave involuntarily) by using force, but you do not deny your recipient an equal right to pursue his own good. Instead, you know that he does not want to get hit by the falling rock, and thus your interference helps him to behave in accordance with his own values. Suppose that a drunken friend wishes to drive home from a party. You and another of his friends realize that he is in no condition to drive. You take his keys, push him into the back seat, and drive him home. The next day he apologizes for his behavior and thanks you for seeing that he got home safely. Again, you did not violate the freedom principle because your interference was consistent with the values of your recipient.

It is important to note that there are paternalistic acts that do not involve the use of force or threats (i.e., coercion). Suppose that Smith is applying to law school and Smith's father is a powerful politician who could use his influence to get his son admitted. Smith asks his father not to interfere; he explains that he does not want to go to law school unless he is admitted on the basis of his own merits. However, Smith's father ignores this request. He discovers that his son will not be admitted unless he uses his influence, and he brings pressure that results in his son's admission. Let us assume that Smith never discovers what his father has done, that he does graduate from law school, and that he goes on to have a successful career as a lawyer. Finally, let us assume that the father's act was paternalistic—his primary motive was to promote his son's welfare. Smith was not coerced, but his father did interfere by causing him to behave involuntarily due to ignorance. Smith would not have chosen to go to law school if he had known that he had been admitted because of his father's influence. Assuming that this decision would have been consistent with Smith's true values, his father has violated the freedom principle.

There are a number of reasons why a person may fail to act in accordance with his own values. A person might be under the influence of a strong emotion such as anger or fear. His rationality might be impaired due to the use of a drug. He might act contrary to his values out of ignorance (e.g., he doesn't know that the bridge he is crossing will collapse). Loss of consciousness may render him unable to act at all. Suppose that Smith takes an unconscious accident victim to the hospital. Unless there is something unusual about this case (e.g., the victim is a devout Christian Scientist), this paternalistic act would not violate the freedom principle.

2.2 In the previous cases, the implications of the freedom principle have been clear. I shall now consider some difficult cases, but first a word of caution. There is a natural tendency to focus on difficult cases because they are usually more interesting. However, when we examine difficult cases, we should not overlook the fact that the freedom principle has clear implications in many other cases. Keeping this word of caution in mind, let us consider the following difficult case. Suppose that a patient requests a specific medicine and his doctor gives him a placebo instead. Let us assume that the doctor knows that the requested medicine would harm the patient. The doctor causes the patient to behave involuntarily by using deception. Does he violate the freedom principle? A "no" answer can be supported by noting that the doctor is seeking to promote the patient's good health, and thus he is helping the patient to pursue the patient's own end. However, we can still ask why it is necessary to deceive the patient. Why doesn't the doctor simply explain to the patient that use of the requested medicine would be harmful? Perhaps he fears that the patient would go to another doctor who would prescribe the medicine, and since his action is consistent with the patient's values (the patient wants to get well), he concludes that his deception is justified. However, we need to know more about the patient in order to know whether the doctor's decision is consistent with the patient's values. In particular, we need to know what value the patient attributes to being self-directing (i.e., to deciding for himself what his own good is and how to *pursue* it). Would the patient prefer to have the freedom to make his own mistakes—even if this results in a period of unnecessary illness?

The following case ups the ante, for we shall assume that a patient's life is at stake. Suppose that a doctor wants to amputate both legs of a seventy-year-old patient with diabetes. If the operation is not performed, the patient will die in a relatively short period of time; however, the patient refuses to give permission for the operation. The doctor seeks and receives a court order granting him the legal right to perform the operation, and he amputates the patient's legs. It may appear that, in this case, we have a clear violation of the freedom principle. Not only is the patient not allowed to be self-directing, but the patient apparently would prefer to die rather than have his legs amputated. Hence, the doctor cannot claim that he is promoting the patient's own end. However, let us introduce a further complication. Suppose that the patient mistakenly believes that he does not face imminent death if his legs are not amputated. When the doctor asks him whether he wants to die, the patient says "no." When the doctor tells him that he will die if his legs are not amputated, the patient does not believe the doctor. Since the patient does not want to die, should we say that the doctor's decision is consistent with the patient's values?

How should we act when we are actually confronted with difficult cases? A good rule of thumb is, when there is doubt about the values of our recipients, we should allow others to be self-directing. In other words, in most cases persons should be allowed to make their own mistakes. One reason for this is that we often learn from our errors; the person who lives a very sheltered life may never learn to take care of himself because he does not profit from the mistakes that he is not allowed to make. One of the insidious things about paternalism is that it feeds upon itself. The more we take care of other persons, the less they are able to take care of themselves, and the more they need our paternalistic concern.

There is another general point to keep in mind when coercive paternalism is contemplated. You may know that a person's life would be better (according to his own values) if he *chooses* to do X. However, it does not follow that his life would be better if he is *compelled* to do X.[1] For one thing, he may resent being coerced, and this resentment may prevent him from understanding that the coercion is (supposedly) for his own good. And this resentment has a reasonable basis. In order to *live* a good life, one must be responsible for one's acts. If the good things in a person's life are the result of coercion, then he cannot take credit for the goodness of his life. A person must be self-directing for *his* life to be good. Hence, a person may resent coercion even in cases in which he must admit that he was compelled to do something good.

These general observations obviously carry less weight when the mistake that a person might make could be fatal. An individual does not learn from his own fatal mistakes, and it is difficult to argue for the overriding value of being self-directing when a person is about to kill himself due to his own ignorance. What should the doctor do with the patient who does not want to die and does not want to have his legs amputated? In my opinion, the freedom principle does not entail a clear answer in this case.

2.3 There are a number of governmental programs that are supposedly justified on paternalistic grounds. A social security program that compels workers to save for their retirement years is an example. Does this program violate the freedom principle? As a general rule, the freedom principle requires noninterference. Since this program is compulsory, it does interfere with workers who would prefer not to participate. However, before we declare that the program violates the freedom principle, we must consider whether any of the exceptions to the noninterference rule apply, (1.2). Self-defense and punishment are irrelevant because the person who refuses to participate in a social security program is not interfering with anyone else. In other words, he is not causing another person to behave involuntarily by using force, threat, or deception, and thus we cannot claim the right to interfere with him on the ground that we are defending someone else's basic right. Paternalism remains as the only possible justification for a compulsory program. The argument for social security on paternalistic grounds is a familiar one. It is claimed that persons would not save for their retirement years unless the government forced them to do so, and thus the government must step in to insure that retired workers have some means of support. One problem with this argument is that it is simply false that *all* persons would fail to provide for their retirement years, and furthermore some persons would prefer to spend their income now and take their chances later on. However, defenders of social security take the position that, since some persons who wish to save lack the self-control to do so, a compulsory program that forces all persons to save is justified. From the standpoint of the freedom principle, this is a classic example of immorality. Some persons are being compelled to participate in a government program in order to insure that others save for their old age. This is an obvious case of some persons using others to further their own ends. I do not dispute that many persons would prefer to have the government force them to save; however, they have no right to compel others to participate in such a program. Our conclusion is clear—compulsory social security programs are immoral.

Occupational licensure is another example of a governmental program that is supposedly justified on paternalistic grounds. Particular occupations are restricted to persons who are granted a license by the government. It is not hard to understand why occupational licensure is advantageous to the persons who have their licenses. It limits competition by limiting entry into the occupations, allowing those who are licensed to charge higher prices for their services. For example, it is doubtful that legislators have passed laws requiring barbers to have a license because irate consumers have demanded protection from incompetent barbers. It is more likely that barbers lobbied for this legislation in order to limit entry into their occupation. If this is the reason for such legislation, then it is clearly immoral. The freedom of some persons is being sacrificed in order to further the ends of others. However, there are occupations for which a stronger case can be made on behalf of paternalistic interference.

Few persons would challenge the claim that only licensed doctors should be allowed to practice medicine. There are at least two important considerations that support this claim. First, consumers are not competent to judge the qualifications of the persons they go to for medical care. It takes years of training to become a competent physician, and only competent physicians are qualified to judge the competence of other doctors. Secondly, incompetent physicians can cause their patients serious harm. The person who gets a bad haircut is not seriously harmed, and he can simply go to a different barber next time. In contrast, the patient who is treated by an incompetent physician may never recover.

Although the arguments for licensing physicians are probably stronger than the arguments for requiring licenses to work at other occupations, I am still not persuaded that licensing is justified. The reason for this is that the freedom principle requires us to take an individual perspective; each person should grant other (individual) persons an equal right to be free. Thus, we must look at particular cases to see whether licensing violates the freedom principle. Suppose that Smith is an acupuncturist and Jones wishes to receive medical treatment from Smith. However, the government prohibits this voluntary interaction because acupuncturists are not licensed to practice medicine. As a general rule, the freedom principle requires noninterference, but again we must consider whether any of the exceptions are relevant. Punishment and self-defense are clearly irrelevant, so paternalism provides the only possible justification for this interference. Paternalistic acts do not violate the freedom principle when the interference is consistent with the recipient's values. But how can the government know that its interference is consistent with Jones's values? Presumably, Jones is seeking treatment because he has a medical problem. And government officials can claim that, since they know that Jones will not receive adequate treatment from an acupuncturist, the interference helps Jones to pursue his end (i.e., good health). However, even if we assume that the government does know that acupuncturists are incompetent physicians, there is still something missing from the government's calculations. How can the government know what value Jones attributes to being self-directing? Perhaps he would insist that he should have the right to make his own mistakes, and thus the government has no right to interfere.

The case for licensure is further weakened when we note that there is a solution that satisfies our paternalistic concern and the demand of the freedom principle. Instead of licensure, the government could institute a program of certification. In this case, the government would certify that individuals have certain skills, but the government would not prohibit noncertified individuals from practicing the occupation. For example, the government would not certify that the acupuncturist is a competent physician, but it would not prohibit him from practicing acupuncture. A program of certification would take care of the problem posed by the consumer's inability to judge the competence of physicians. Jones would know that Smith has not been certified as a competent physician, but Jones's right to be self-directing would still be respected, for he would have the freedom to choose to be treated by Smith.[2]

A program of certification gives consumers the information that they supposedly lack, while, at the same time, consumers are granted the freedom to receive services from non-certified individuals. Such programs would not violate the freedom principle as long as they were not financed by coercive taxes. Instead, those individuals who wish to be certified should pay a fee that covers the administrative costs of the program. This procedure would have the advantage of discouraging the proliferation of frivolous certification programs. Barbers, for example, would be likely to seek certification only if there would be an economic advantage in being certified. And whether a certified barber could charge more for his services would depend on whether consumers want the "protection" of going to certified barbers.

Paternalistic arguments are often given in support of government regulation of the sale and use of drugs. However, the selective use of paternalistic arguments should raise some doubts about the sincerity of those who employ them. Drugs like nicotine, caffeine, and alcohol are known to be harmful to many users, but one rarely hears the paternalists advocate more comprehensive regulation of their use. One possible reason for imposing severe restrictions on the use of some harmful drugs is that certain drugs are *more* harmful than others. I shall examine this reason by considering whether the sale and use of heroin should be prohibited.

It is difficult to get reliable information on the effects of heroin use. However, we do know that heroin is addictive and that users sometimes die from heroin overdose. The person who stops using an addictive drug suffers physical discomfort. Alcohol, caffeine, nicotine, and heroin are addictive drugs. Presumably what distinguishes heroin from the other three is that heroin is *more* addictive; the person who stops using heroin suffers severe withdrawal symptoms. However, it is important to note that heroin users can quit. (For example, many American soldiers who used heroin in Viet-Nam quit using the drug when they returned to the States.) How can we measure the strength of a physical addiction? I have known cigarette smokers who claim that they cannot quit. This claim requires interpretation. What they really mean is that it is very difficult to quit, and they do not have enough incentive to make the effort. Likewise, heroin users can quit, but in some cases, they may require help. I shall return to this point shortly.

Is the fact that some heroin users kill themselves by overdosing a sufficient reason for prohibiting the use of the drug? As we have previously noted, the freedom principle requires that we examine such questions from an individual perspective—we should grant each (individual) person an equal right to be free. Suppose that Jones is a heroin user who does not want to quit using the drug. A law that prohibits Jones from using heroin because other users are killing themselves by overdosing would violate Jones's basic right. Such a law would restrict one person's freedom in order to promote the ends of other persons, and thus it violates the injunction against using persons "as a mere means."

Suppose that Smith is a heroin user who does not want to quit, but he lacks the will power to do so without help. This would be a case in which paternalism does not violate the freedom principle because the interference is consistent with Smith's values. Smith's wife, for example, could justifiably seek a court order committing Smith to an institution where he would receive help in withdrawing from the drug. There are undoubtedly many cases in which paternalistic interference with heroin users would be justified. However, an advocate of the freedom principle cannot support a general prohibition of heroin use, for such a law would violate the basic right of heroin users who value using the drug.

This discussion has been limited to paternalistic reasons for prohibiting the use of heroin. I shall discuss another reason for prohibiting its use (the crime problem) in the next chapter, (3.7). Let us conclude this section by considering what should be done if new information is forthcoming about the harmful effects of heroin use. For example, suppose it is determined that heroin is a carcinogen. The obvious libertarian position would be that there is no reason to treat heroin any differently than cigarettes. Persons should be informed that heroin is a carcinogen, and they should be allowed to make their own decisions about whether to use the drug.

2.4 The category of persons includes both actual and potential self-directing agents. Why does the freedom principle apply to potential self-directing agents? The reason for this is that it would be arbitrary to exclude potential self-directing agents. The potential self-directing agent, given normal development, will become an autonomous agent. He lacks the capacity for autonomous action now, but he will acquire this capacity in the future. And if we should respect human beings because of their capacity for autonomous action, we should respect human beings who will have this capacity. As Alan Donagan notes:

> The principle underlying this reasoning is: if respect is owed to beings because they are in a certain state, it is owed to whatever, by its very nature, develops into that state. To reject this principle would be arbitrary, if indeed it would be intelligible.[3]

The capacity for autonomous action is valuable now, and it will be valuable in the future, and thus those who will develop this capacity deserve our moral respect.

I have already argued that the duty to care for children falls on the natural parents, (1.4). Since the parents have produced a helpless person, they have a duty to care for their offspring until he is able to care for himself. If a child dies because of parental neglect, the parents would be guilty of killing their child. Parental care includes paternalistic acts to promote the child's welfare. According to our rule, paternalistic acts do not violate the freedom principle when the interference is consistent with the recipient's own values. However, this rule does not apply to young children since they have no values.

There is a difference between wanting *x* and valuing *x*. Young children have many wants, but they do not have values. Young children are naive egoists; they want immediate gratification. One of the problems with this is that their desires often conflict. For example, most young children want to eat lots of candy, and they also want to be healthy. If given the opportunity, they will eat lots of candy. This does not mean that they value the pleasure of eating candy more than they value good health. They are simply unable to establish priorities by taking a long-range point of view; they want *immediate* gratification. A major reason for their lack of values is the lack of a clear conception of time. The young child cannot make plans for the future because he is unable to conceive of what his life can be like five years from now—or even one year from now. To have values, a person must be able to conceive of future alternatives. He must be able to understand that he can be this or that type of person, do this or that kind of activity in the future. He must also be able to recognize conflicting desires so that he can establish priorities among them. Finally, to act on his values, he must have the self-control to resist the impulse to seek immediate gratification when it conflicts with the satisfaction of more important desires.

I am using the expression 'having values' in the neutral sense in which no judgment is made about whether the values are good or bad. The heroin addict, for example, can value using heroin. Its use may conflict with other desires the addict has, but he may believe that the pleasure derived from using heroin is more important than satisfying other desires. When I say that the child does not really value eating lots of candy, I am not claiming that eating lots of candy could not be valuable. Rather, I claim that young children cannot have any values because they lack the necessary conceptual abilities. They are unable to conceive of future alternatives, and thus they cannot appreciate conflicts among their desires.

The freedom principle is violated when a person is denied an equal right to pursue his own good. Since young children have no values, paternalistic acts directed at them do not violate the freedom principle. Furthermore, since parents have a duty to care for their children, they often have a positive duty to act paternalistically. However, parents must remember that their ultimate objective should be to help children develop into autonomous agents who are responsible for their own welfare.

Children become autonomous agents by a long and slow process in which they acquire the necessary cognitive skills and develop self-control. There is no obvious point at which time a child can be said to pass from the condition of being a potential autonomous agent to the condition of being an actual autonomous agent. This can be a source of moral perplexity because the extent to which we are required to respect a child's equal right to be free may not be clear. Suppose, for example, that a twelve-year-old says he does not want to go to school. His desire to do x (drop out of school) does not show that he really values doing x. There are obvious reasons for doubting that a twelve-year-old has real values with respect to this issue. It is doubtful that he truly knows what he wants to do in the future, and thus it is doubtful that he can appreciate the value of an education. Even if he is able to establish priorities between conflicting desires, he may not have the self-control to resist the impulse to seek immediate gratification. On the other hand, it is both dangerous and probably wrong to assume that twelve-year-olds have no real values. A libertarian in particular should be troubled by such a general claim because narrow-minded parents may use this claim to "justify" extreme forms of coercive paternalism.

There are no easy answers in this area, but I have already discussed some factors to keep in mind when one is faced with a difficult case, (2.2). In general, assuming that mistakes will inevitably be made (by parents and children), it is better for parents to err on the side of being too permissive rather than being too restrictive. Children often learn by making mistakes; the child who leads a very sheltered life may never become a responsible person because he does not profit from the experience acquired by taking risks. Also, most mistakes that children make are not fatal, and thus they have the opportunity to recover from them, and in many cases they can rectify them.

As a general rule, the younger the child the more likely it is that paternalistic interference will not violate the freedom principle. For example, it is reasonable to assume that parents have the right to compel an eight-year-old to go to school. But does the state have the right to compel parents to send their children to school? Such a law would presumably be based on a paternalistic concern for children. However, it is important to note that the law interferes with the parents' freedom of choice. Is this interference consistent with the freedom principle? Since each (individual) person has an equal right to be free, we must look at individual cases to answer this question. Suppose that Amish parents do not want to send their child to school. They believe that public schools are breeding grounds of bad habits and immoral behavior. (This is not an unreasonable belief given the sorry state of public schools in many areas of the United States.) Furthermore, they do not have enough money to send their child to a private school. As a result, they educate the child at home, and they teach the child (among other things) to read, to write, and to do basic arithmetic. Let us also assume that the child is well-fed, well-clothed, etc., and thus the parents are fulfilling their duty to take care of the child until he is able to care for himself. In this case, a law requiring Amish parents to send their child to school would violate the freedom principle.

It is often argued that literacy is a necessity in a modern society, and as a result, the state must require that children attend school. This argument confuses schooling with education. As Murray Rothbard notes:

> Education is a lifelong process of learning, and learning takes place not only in school, but in all areas of life. When the child plays, or listens to parents or friends, or reads a newspaper, or works at a job, he or she is becoming *educated*. Formal schooling is only a

small part of the educational process, and is really only suitable for formal subjects of instruction, particularly in the more advanced and systematic subjects. The elementary subjects, reading, writing, arithmetic and their corollaries, can easily be learned at home and outside the school.[4]

Many persons probably believe that there would be disastrous consequences if compulsory schooling were abolished. However, if schooling is so valuable, most parents will surely realize this and they will send their children to school. Most parents care about their children, and they do not need the state to tell them to act in the best interest of their offspring.

But what about the (presumably) rare case in which parents do not send their child to school and they do not teach him to read or write at home? Even in this case, there is no reason to assume that the consequences will be disastrous. Suppose, for example, that Jones is a sixteen-year-old who does not know how to read or write. He has various odd jobs like delivering papers. Suppose that he uses some of his money to take a reading class. Learning to read is not that difficult, and once one learns to read, self-education becomes possible. Thus, we should not assume that illiteracy is the inevitable outcome of the failure of parents to provide a formal education for their children.[5] We also should not assume that a child who does not receive a formal education will be condemned to a life of poverty. There are many examples of individuals who have acquired great wealth even though they had very little schooling. Furthermore, in a free society, wages would be determined by supply and demand (see 6.2), and thus we cannot know in advance what the incomes of various workers would be. For example, if many persons want to be college teachers, the average income of teachers could be lower than the average income of sanitation workers, barbers, or plumbers.

From a libertarian point of view, compulsory schooling laws should be abolished. Having a family and raising children are ways in which persons seek to give meaning to their lives. As long as parents do not violate the rights of others, no one has the right to interfere with these activities. The parental right to raise children includes the right to decide what schooling (if any) a young child will receive. In the United States, teachers' unions would surely fight any attempt to abolish compulsory schooling laws. However, teachers have no right to use others as a mere means in order to promote their own end (i.e., job security). And given the conditions in many public schools, it is surely immoral to require parents to send their children to such schools, (see 6.6).

2.5 The parental right to raise children is limited by the qualification that parents should not violate the rights of others—including the rights of their children. As a result, there are some decisions that parents do not have the right to make. Consider the case in which Smith's son will die unless he receives medical care. However, Smith, who is a devout Christian Scientist, refuses to give permission for the necessary treatment. In this case, interference to save the child's life would be justified. Smith has no right to impose his religious beliefs on his son, and furthermore, he is violating his duty to care for his child until the child is able to care for himself.

Children are not the property of their parents. Each child is a distinct individual with his own life to lead and his own rights. Among these rights are the right to parental care, and when this right is violated, others can justifiably step in to see that the child is taken care of. In some cases, the government would even be justified in taking children away from their parents. This should be done only in extreme cases of neglect or physical cruelty. As with all criminal matters, the burden of proof lies with the state, and thus the evidence against the parents should be compelling, (see 3.5).

For libertarians who are anarchists, child abuse presents a serious problem. Anarchists assume that persons will hire private protection agencies to protect them from crime. However, it is unrealistic to assume that a child can hire a protection agency to protect him from parental abuse. I shall say more about the problems of anarchism in the next chapter, (3.2).

Chapter Three

Punishment

3.1 My main objective in this chapter is to develop a theory of legal punishment. As a first step, I shall establish that there are cases in which punishment does not violate the freedom principle. Then I shall argue that the state should punish lawbreakers. Once this groundwork is laid, I shall discuss some practical proposals for implementing the theory.

Let us begin by noting that there are cases in which self-defense does not violate the freedom principle. Suppose that A attacks B and B uses physical force to repel the attack. For example, B might knock A to the ground and hold him down while onlookers summon the police. In this case, B is not assuming that he has a superior right to be free; he is simply defending his equal right to be free by preventing a relationship in which he is treated as if he were inferior. Furthermore, B does not violate A's rights since A has no right to attack B. We should also note that, since B has the right to defend himself, other persons have the right to help B defend himself.

Self-defense differs from punishment because (by definition) only the interference necessary to defend oneself is used, while in cases of punishment, the offender is penalized for his transgression. Why do we have the right to punish an offender *after* the offense has been committed? To answer this question, let us imagine a very simple legal system that has one law—a law prohibiting assault. Let us stipulate that this law prescribes a three month prison term as punishment for assault. The rationale behind this threat of punishment is that potential victims of assaults have the right to have others respect their equal right to be free, and, as a result, they have the concomitant right to protect themselves by using the threat of punishment to deter potential assailants. In this case, they are not claiming a superior right to be free; they are simply trying to get others to respect their *equal* right to be free. Ideally, every person would respect the basic right of others, and thus no assaults would occur and no punishment would be inflicted. However, let us assume that A, who is well aware of the law prohibiting assault, still chooses to assault B. If A is subsequently punished, he will have no ground for claiming that his equal right to be free has not been respected. A could have avoided the punishment by refraining from doing what he had no right to do in the first place. Thus, A brings the punishment on himself by choosing not to respect the basic right of another person.

Looking at this issue in more general terms, legal punishment does not violate the freedom principle when two conditions are met:

(1) The law prohibits acts that violate the freedom principle (which means that the offender had no right to perform the act).

(2) The offender could have avoided the punishment by choosing not to break the law.

In other words, the two conditions are met when the offender could have avoided the threatened punishment by choosing not to do what he had no right to do.

3.2 I shall now argue that legal punishment is preferrable (in most cases) to the alternative methods of dealing with offenders. One alternative is anarchism. In an anarchistic society, there would be no government to make and enforce laws. A naive response to this alternative is to assume that there would be an increase in crime. However, individuals in an anarchistic society would certainly take steps to protect themselves. We can assume, for example, that many persons would employ the services of private protection agencies. And anarchists claim that, since private protection agencies must compete for customers, they would do a better job of protecting their clients' rights than the law enforcement agencies run by the government.

If private protection agencies are likely to be more efficient than their governmental counterparts, what is wrong with anarchism? Let us begin to answer this question by noting that there are problems with the claim that private protection agencies would protect their customers' rights. What rights do their customers have? The anarchist needs a moral theory to answer this question, and assuming that there are good reasons for accepting it (see 7.4), the freedom principle should be used in determining what rights individuals have.

According to the freedom principle, what can protection agencies do? They can come to the aid of their customers *while* their clients are being victimized. These customers have the right of self-defense, and others (e.g., a protection agency) can help them defend their basic right. However, in cases in which interference is justified on the ground of self-defense, a protection agency should use only the force (or the threat of force) that is necessary to defend its clients' basic right. Hence, this sort of activity may have little deterrent effect.

Do protection agencies have the right to punish offenders who violate their customers' rights? They do *if* certain conditions are met. An offender should not be punished unless he had the opportunity to avoid the punishment by choosing not to violate the rules of the protection agency, (3.1). To satisfy this requirement, protection agencies must publicize the rules of their punishment systems. Surely no attempt would be made to punish all violations of their customers' rights, and thus protection agencies must state in advance which violations are serious enough to be punishable offenses, (see 3.5). Protection agencies must also publicize the particular punishments that will be inflicted for particular offenses. It should be apparent that these requirements point to a serious problem. A potential offender cannot be expected to know which agency is protecting this or that person, and he cannot be expected to know what the rules are for the various punishment systems of the different agencies.

To summarize, the potential offender has the right to know what risk (in terms of possible punishment) he is taking if he violates another person's rights. Ex post facto "laws" violate the freedom principle; thus the rules of a punishment system should be made known in advance. However, if different protection agencies have different rules, there will be many cases in which it would be unreasonable to assume that an offender ought to have known what risk he was taking. It is at least conceivable that protection agencies could deal with this problem by agreeing on one set of rules governing which violations are punishable offenses and the specific punishments assigned to each.

Another serious problem arises because "justice" is bought in this system. For example, suppose that the Strongarm Protection Agency arrests Smith for shoplifting in a branch of Goliath Stores. Smith is actually innocent, but Goliath has an interest in securing his conviction since he would serve as an example to persons who might be tempted to shoplift. Goliath is also the major customer of Strongarm Protection Agency. If Smith's rights are to be protected, Strongarm must follow procedures that are likely to produce an impartial verdict.

Suppose that Smith is convicted by Strongarm. However, Smith is a client of a protection agency, the Fairness Agency. Fairness does not believe that its client was treated fairly. It rejects Strongarm's procedures in general and objects to the particular application of procedures used in Smith's case. Furthermore, the Fairness Agency is convinced that its client is innocent. Fairness and Strongarm could resolve their differences by fighting, but this would be a costly solution for firms that are interested in making profits. Let us imagine that they agree to let an arbitrator resolve their disputes. The arbitrator will rule on the general procedures of Strongarm as well as the application of particular procedures. If the arbitrator is to make rulings that are consistent with the freedom principle, he must insist that procedures be used that are likely to insure that innocent persons are not punished. Furthermore, the procedures must reflect the fact that the freedom principle requires the recognition of excusing conditions. We have the right to punish only if the offender had the opportunity *to choose* not to commit the offense, (see 3.5). When an offender has no real choice due to coercion, ignorance, mental illness, etc., he should be excused.

To summarize, protection agencies must publicize the rules of their punishment systems; they must state which violations of the freedom principle are punishable offences and what the punishments are. To secure convictions, they must use impartial procedures that safeguard the rights of the accused. This sounds like "the rule of law," and it is generally held that it is the business of government to establish the rule of law. If this view can be defended, we will have demonstrated that government should be the dominant protection agency, which means that the government will have the task of insuring that individuals and other protection agencies abide by the rule of law.

Why should government assume responsibility for establishing the rule of law? Many violations of the freedom principle involve violations of property rights. To decide which violations of property rights should be punishable offenses, we must first establish what property rights individuals have. A major part of this task involves deciding who has the right to use which resources. Resources are things that are valuable for human use but are not produced by human beings. Land, water, fossil fuels, and mineral deposits are examples. Since resources are not produced by human beings, no individuals have an obvious claim on them. I shall argue in the next chapter that decisions concerning who has the right to use resources should be made by democratic political procedures. Hence, no individuals (or their protection agencies) have the right to establish their own property rules for resources. I conclude that a democratic government should establish the rule of law, and this entails that the anarchistic "solution" to the crime problem must be rejected.

3.3 Some writers maintain that legal punishment is a barbaric legacy that should be replaced by more "scientific" methods of dealing with offenders. They claim that offenders should be *treated* rather than punished.[1] Let us assume that the following proposal covers the main features of the treatment alternative:

> After a person has been convicted of a crime, he is examined by a team of psychiatrists who make a professional judgment as to whether the offender continues to have antisocial tendencies. If they judge that the offender no longer has antisocial tendencies, then he is simply released. If the psychiatrists judge that the offender continues to have antisocial tendencies, then he may be sent to an institution where he can receive treatment, or he may receive treatment without being institutionalized. In either case, the treatment stops when the offender is cured of his antisocial tendencies.

There is an obvious reason for doubting that treatment is a genuine alternative to punishment. The treatment will usually be involuntary, and thus the offender suffers a loss of freedom in most cases. However, there is an important difference between treatment and punishment. In a treatment system, if the psychiatrists decide that a lawbreaker exhibits no further antisocial tendencies, he is set free. For example, suppose that Jones murders his wife because he hates her. The psychiatrists decide that

Jones had good reasons for hating his wife and that he does not pose a threat to anyone else, and thus they release him. In contrast, in a just punishment system, the penalty for premeditated murder (e.g., 15 to 25 years in prison) would be clearly stated, and Jones would receive the specified punishment—regardless of whether he still posed a danger to others.

There are many problems with the treatment alternative to punishment. For example, there is the obvious danger of political abuse. Suppose that Smith commits an act of civil disobedience, and the psychiatrists decide that he continues to exhibit antisocial tendencies due to his political beliefs. What is the cure? Do government employees have the right to try to change a person's political beliefs? The totalitarian possibilities of such a practice are frightening. In the Soviet Union, political dissidents are often placed in mental institutions to be "cured." This is an example that a libertarian society should not emulate.

Those who engage in civil disobedience may not be "mentally ill" in any ordinary sense of that phrase. Likewise, ordinary criminals may not be mentally ill either, and thus the notion of a "cure" becomes problematic. Consider the case of the house burglar who steals primarily because he can make more money as a burglar than by working at the legitimate jobs for which he is qualified. He also finds ordinary jobs to be boring; he has had several different jobs, but he has always gone back to burglary in part because he missed the excitement. What is the cure? Should the government give him a high paying, exciting job at the taxpayers' expense? If not, suppose that there is only one known "cure"—psychosurgery which will result in a very passive and dependent individual. This example raises the problem of cruel and unusual treatment.

In a treatment system, the psychiatrist who can cure an offender only by using extreme measures such as heavy drug dosage or psychosurgery faces a dilemma. The method used to cure the offender is objectionable, but the offender who is not cured must be detained indefinitely. The indefinite sentence is a crucial aspect of the treatment alternative. The psychiatrist is not punishing the lawbreaker for his past offense; his job is to "cure," and the offender is not released until he is cured. There are many problems with indefinite sentences. For one thing, an indefinite sentence seems much too extreme for most crimes. In a treatment system, a burglar, for example, could spend the rest of his life in an institution if he fails to respond to treatment. On the other hand, another burglar who responds to treatment might be released in a few months. This suggests problems with respect to justice; persons committing the same crimes could receive very different sentences. A treatment system gives far too much discretionary power to the psychiatrists who determine whether, and when, an offender is released. There is far too much latitude for racism, prejudice, and stupidity to flourish. For example, an offender may fail to respond to treatment because he is given the wrong treatment and, as a result, he could be institutionalized indefinitely.

We can also question whether involuntary treatment will work. Surely, treatment is most likely to be successful when the patient seeks help. In an involuntary setting, a patient may not cooperate with the psychiatrists. A non-cooperating patient can be threatened with indefinite detention, but this is likely to produce another unhappy result—the offender will fake cooperation in order to secure his release.

Even if we ignore the previous criticisms, there is still a fatal objection to the treatment alternative. Psychiatrists do not have sufficient knowledge to make a treatment system work. They do not know enough about the causes of criminal behavior, and they do not know how to "cure" many antisocial behavior patterns. Because of my belief in human autonomy, I hold that normal human beings will never be sufficiently predictable or malleable for a treatment system to work—unless morally objectionable treatments like heavy drug dosage or psychosurgery are commonly used. Subsequent events may prove that my views about the limitations of psychiatry are only prejudices, but for now at least treatment is not a realistic alternative to punishment.

3.4 Let us now look at restitution as a possible alternative to legal punishment. The basic assumption of restitution is that the victim of a crime deserves compensation from the offender. The victim has suffered a loss, and justice requires that the offender make restitution for the loss he has caused.

There are some obvious practical problems with restitution. For one thing, when an offender commits a murder there is no victim left to compensate. A more common difficulty will arise when offenders are ordered to pay monetary compensation. We can expect that many offenders will not have regular jobs, and thus they will lack a normal source of income from which they can pay compensation. As a result, they may commit further crimes in order to acquire the money. It has been suggested that unemployed offenders who cannot pay compensation should be assigned to work projects.[2] However, if these offenders are not institutionalized, they may commit further crimes. On the other hand, if they are institutionalized, the cost of maintaining security plus the cost of room and board may well exceed the income that the offender *earns.* We can expect that many of the offenders who must be institutionalized will not be highly skilled and productive workers.

Another important objection is that the penalties imposed in a restitution system may have little or no deterrent effect. The obvious example of this is the rich person who can easily compensate the victims of his crimes. A wealthy person who is sadistic could hire thugs to assault his enemies. If the crimes are traced back to their source, the wealthy offender could satisfy his legal liabilities by paying court costs and compensating his victims. To cite another example, suppose that Jones is an incompetent car thief who is caught on the average once every ten times that he steals a car. What is the penalty? He obviously has to return the car. Suppose that he is ordered to pay the victim $1000 as compensation for the victim's inconvenience and mental distress. Let us also assume that he must pay court costs, so he pleads guilty to keep the costs down, and he pays an additional $1000. To summarize, the price of getting caught is $2000. However, since he is caught only once every ten times, he can treat the $2000 as a business expense that he can cover by stealing another car.

Most crimes are not solved, and thus most victims will not be compensated in a restitution system. Furthermore, it is not just the immediate victims who are hurt by crime. We all pay avoidance costs. People buy locks, burglar alarms, guard dogs, etc. We pay for police protection. Businesses hire security personnel, and the cost is passed on to the consumer. Many persons buy insurance to protect themselves from financial loss due to crime, and many persons restrict their activities because of crime. The rapist, for example, harms other persons besides his immediate victims. The woman who stays home at night because she fears being attacked is also harmed. Crime can have a very divisive influence on society, and if the crime rate becomes excessive, social living is impossible. Thus, it is vitally important that the penalties for criminal acts have some deterrent effect.

A defender of restitution might argue that the lack of deterrence problem can be dealt with by more severe penalties. However, this solution goes beyond the restitution paradigm. Restitution (as an alternative to punishment) is based on the view that the victim should be compensated by the offender. Whether this causes the offender to suffer or whether it deters anyone else is irrelevant. Restitution is only concerned with doing justice to the victim; it is not concerned with the suppression of crime. If deterrence is a consideration in determining penalties, then we have a punishment system—not a restitution system.

3.5 I have argued that there are cases in which punishment does not violate the freedom principle. I have also argued that the alternatives to legal punishment are unacceptable. These arguments and their conclusions establish the basic framework for a libertarian theory of legal punishment. I shall now consider some practical proposals for implementing the theory.

Let us begin by noting that there are obvious reasons for not making *all* violations of the freedom principle punishable offenses. Law enforcement is costly, and in some cases the benefits may be so slight that they do not warrant the cost. In some cases, only severe punishments would have a deterrent effect, and we may judge that the offense is not serious enough to justify severe punishments. In other cases, law enforcement would require unacceptable invasions of privacy. For example, a government effort to make all promisors keep their promises would result in massive interference in the private lives of citizens.

Teleological values such as costliness and deterrence will play a role in decisions about which violations of the freedom principle should be punishable offenses. A critic might object that lawmakers are assuming that they have a superior right to be free when they decide that some violations will be illegal and others will not. The answer to this objection is that, in a just system of punishment, the penalties for illegal behavior are publicized. Hence, when an offender breaks a law, he knows (or at least he should have known) that he can be punished for his offense. Not only does he choose to violate the freedom principle; he also chooses to run the risk of punishment.

A just system of punishment must allow persons to determine their legal liabilities by the choices they make. When a person's illegal behavior is unintentional, he should be excused. Mistakes, accidents, and ignorance should be recognized as possible excusing conditions.[3] There are also cases in which coercion may be a legitimate excuse. Suppose that Brown is stopped at an intersection and a bank robber jumps in his car, pushes a gun in his ribs, and demands that Brown drive him to a particular address. If Brown helps the robber by complying with this demand, Brown should be excused because he had no real choice. There are also cases in which offenders should be excused due to mental illness or mental incompetence. This excuse introduces notorious practical difficulties, but in theory at least it is clear what we should look for. Did the offender know that he was behaving illegally, and was he capable of controlling his behavior? In most cases, the offender who takes obvious precautions to avoid being caught should not be excused. Such an offender knows that he is breaking the law, and his precautionary actions indicate that he is in control of his behavior.

Some persons should be excused because of their age. When a three-year-old picks up a loaded gun and shoots his brother, he should be excused. This is a clear case, but there will be other cases in which it is not so clear whether age is a legitimate excuse. What should be done with an eight-year-old who shoots his brother? Again, in theory at least, we know what to look for. Did the child know that his behavior was illegal and that he could be punished for the offense? And was he in control of his behavior? Even if the eight-year-old knew that his behavior was illegal, we may have doubts about his ability to control his behavior. Thus, it is likely that he should not be held fully responsible; his age is (at least) a mitigating factor which should be taken into account if a decision is made to punish.

Since human beings are fallible, no punishment system will be immune from mistakes. Inevitably, persons who should be excused, and some who have not violated the freedom principle, will be punished. Such mistakes may lead a skeptic to conclude that all systems of legal punishment must violate the freedom principle. We know that some individuals will be unjustly punished. If we continue to punish in spite of this knowledge, because we want to deter potential lawbreakers, then we will be using these persons as a mere means in order to promote our end (deterrence).

There is an analogous argument for skepticism in epistemology. Crudely put, the argument claims that since we are fallible beings we can never be certain that any belief is true. Few philosophers find this argument to be persuasive. For example, I believe that I am looking at my pen. How do I know that my belief is not mistaken? The object that I am looking at looks like my pen. It feels like a pen. It writes like a pen. Furthermore, there is simply no reason to doubt that it is a pen; and therefore, I can justifiably conclude that I know that I am looking at my pen. And the fact that my beliefs are sometimes false gives me no reason *in this case* to think that I could be mistaken. Likewise, if I see Jones commit a crime, I have no reason to doubt that he did commit a crime.

Skepticism about the right to punish, based on human fallibility, does show us why the state must assume a heavy burden of proof. If we punish a person when there is reasonable doubt about his guilt, then he might be innocent and we would be violating the injunction against using the person as a mere means. Thus, we should punish only if we are certain "beyond a reasonable doubt" that the offender is guilty.

3.6 What are the appropriate punishments for particular crimes? This is a difficult question to answer because we often must weigh two conflicting values: deterrence and justice. The purpose of the threat of punishment is to deter potential lawbreakers. As a general rule, we would expect severe punishments to have greater deterrent effect. For example, if the penalty for shoplifting were twenty years in prison, we would expect that few persons would take this risk. However, most persons would hold that a twenty year sentence for shoplifting is unjust because it is too severe. Ideally, punishments should "fit" the crime in the sense that the severity of punishment corresponds to the gravity of the offense. If lawbreakers receive severe penalties for minor offenses, they will not get their just deserts.[4]

In cases involving serious offenses, there is no conflict between the values of deterrence and justice. For example, most violent crimes are serious offenses. When there is serious injury (or even the risk of serious injury), we have a serious crime, and severe penalties would be appropriate in terms of both justice and deterrence. Another relevant fact is that most violent crimes are committed by young males. If these offenders are incarcerated for long periods of time, they will be older and hence less likely to commit further violent crimes when they are released.

The gravity of monetary crimes will usually correspond to the financial loss of the victim; the greater the financial loss the more serious the offense. This consideration helps us in ranking crimes according to their gravity, and such a ranking helps in determining severity of punishment. Ideally, we should also have factual information about the deterrent effect of different penalties for different crimes. This would help us in determining, for example, whether capital punishment is the appropriate punishment for premeditated murder. At the other end of the scale, such information would also help in determining what the penalties should be for crimes like vandalism and shoplifting.

Whatever penalties are ultimately decided upon, justice requires that they be determinate and well-publicized. In order to conclude that lawbreakers deserve their punishments, persons should be able to determine their legal liabilities by their own choices. Hence, potential lawbreakers should have the opportunity to find out what punishment they are risking if they choose to commit an offense. These considerations point to serious problems with the common practice of plea bargaining. The objective of plea bargaining (from the prosecutor's point of view) is to secure a guilty plea from the accused. In return, the accused is given special consideration which usually consists of a reduced charge and, as a result, a less severe punishment. As one writer has noted, plea bargaining *systematically* produces unjust results.[5] If we assume that the legally prescribed penalties for particular offenses are just, then just verdicts will never result from plea bargaining—except by accident. The guilty defendant who pleads guilty to a lesser charge will receive a less severe penalty than is appropriate for his (actual) offense. For example, a rapist who pleads guilty to assault may get probation instead of five years in prison. An innocent defendant who pleads guilty will obviously not get what he deserves, i.e., acquittal. A further injustice is perpetrated because some defendants are allowed to plea bargain and some are not. Thus, lawbreakers who commit the same offense may receive very different punishments.

Another problem with plea bargaining is that the "bargaining" takes place in a coercive situation in which the accused is offered a choice between a more severe punishment of uncertain probability and a less severe punishment. The threat of a possible punishment of greater severity may cause an innocent defendant to plead guilty. This is particularly true of poor defendants who cannot afford an elaborate defense or who cannot post bail. Because of the backlog of cases in many legal jurisdictions, a defendant who cannot post bail may secure his freedom more quickly by pleading guilty. This presents a temptation that an innocent defendant may be unable to resist.

There is an obvious practical objection to doing away with plea bargaining. Due to the large backlog of cases in many legal jurisdictions, it would be very difficult to decide more cases by jury trial. The abolition of victimless crimes would undoubtedly help our overcrowded court system, (see 3.7). More courts and prosecutors would also help. If this is not enough, perhaps we should think of alternatives to the jury trial. The jury trial provides many valuable safeguards. However, if we must choose between (1) settling most cases by plea bargaining while a few cases are decided by jury trial and (2) abolishing plea bargaining and finding an alternative to the jury trial, I think that justice would be better served by the latter.[6]

3.7 Illegal gambling, prostitution, the sale and use of illicit drugs, and the sale of pornography are often called victimless crimes. It is sometimes said that victimless crimes are crimes in which no one is harmed. The obvious problem with this claim is that the participants in these crimes are often harmed. For example, the drug user may be harmed by his use of drugs; the gambler who loses money may be harmed; the customer who gets venereal disease from a prostitute is harmed, etc. In light of these obvious counterexamples, the claim that no one is harmed is often amended to state that "no one else" is harmed, i.e., no person other than the participants is harmed. But again this claim does not survive the evidence. For example, the friends or family of the drug user may be harmed by his condition; some persons who oppose prostitution are harmed by the mental distress they suffer by knowing that prostitution exists; the family of the gambler may be harmed, etc. We must conclude that victimless crimes cannot be characterized by a lack of harm. To clarify what I mean when I use the expression 'victimless crime,' I shall stipulate that we have a victimless crime when an activity is illegal even though there is *no interference,* i.e., no one causes another person to behave involuntarily by using force, threat, or deception.[7]

The freedom principle entails that victimless crimes should be abolished. Since the participants in these "crimes" do not cause other persons to behave involuntarily, the government cannot claim that these laws are needed to defend the basic right of others. Paternalism remains as the only exception to the noninterference rule that could justify prohibiting these activities. However, while paternalism might justify interference in particular cases, it cannot justify a *general* prohibition of these activities. For example, suppose that lawmakers claim that the law prohibiting prostitution is justified in order to prevent prostitutes and their customers from getting venereal disease. The problem here is that there are prostitutes and customers who would prefer to take this risk. Hence, the lawmakers are violating the freedom principle by imposing their values on others.[8]

Let us now consider a case that points to a problem for libertarian theory. Suppose that Jones places a billboard on the roof of his theatre for the purpose of advertising a pornographic movie. Let us also assume that the billboard has a graphic scene from the movie, and many persons think that the advertisement is obscene. The showing of a pornographic movie is a private activity; only those who wish to need participate. However, the billboard is public, and thus it will be seen by many persons who would prefer not to see it. Should this kind of advertising be prohibited?

Let us analyze this problem by examining the following assumptions:

(1) There should be at least some laws enforcing standards of public decency.

(2) No activities are indecent "by their very nature."

If (1) is rejected, the problem dissolves. However, there are limits to the tolerance of most persons; even very liberal persons can probably think of some public activities that they would want to prohibit. If public nudity does not offend, what about sexual acts performed in public? Or sadistic-masochistic sexual activities? Or defecation in public? When confronted with offensive activities, a person can avert his eyes. The persons who do not want to see Jones's billboard can use another street. But why should *they* have to restrict their activities in this way. Furthermore, it is clear that some laws enforcing standards of public decency do not violate the freedom principle. Consider the case of Smith who likes to shout obscenities while standing on the sidewalk near a busy intersection. Smith violates the freedom principle by forcing others to listen to his obscene language. Does Jones also violate the freedom principle? One might argue that Jones is using his own property, and therefore no one has the right to compel him to remove the picture from his billboard. However, as we shall see in the next chapter, this view of property rights is too simple.

The second assumption (2) is based on the view that what is considered obscene or indecent is primarily the result of social conditioning. For example, bathing suits that would have been thought scandalous fifty years ago are now considered very modest. If such views are the result of social conditioning, then there is no way to determine *a priori* that something is indecent. Something is indecent only if people *in fact* think it is indecent. If persons did not consider public nudity on swimming beaches to be indecent, for example, then it would not be.

The problem of public decency is difficult for the libertarian because there is a clash of freedoms. Should persons have the right to do things in public that others consider indecent? Should persons have the right to use public streets, parks, etc. without being confronted with activities that they consider indecent? The answer in some cases is clear. When Smith shouts obscenities, he violates the freedom principle by forcing others to listen, and thus we have the right to prohibit this activity. Does

Jones force others to view his billboard? If a person uses another street to avoid seeing it, is he responding to a threat? Assuming that there are no clear answers to these questions, perhaps the best that can be done is to establish a procedure for deciding such cases. A democratic political procedure gives each citizen the right to have a say in what standards of public decency will be enforced. Such a procedure has the danger that the majority will vote for politicians who favor repressive laws. However, in a libertarian society this danger is mitigated because there would be no restrictions on what persons do in private. There would be no censorship of books, magazines, films, radio, or television. Thus, a puritanical majority, for example, cannot control the dissemination of liberal ideas. It is also likely that the members of a libertarian society will value freedom, and thus it is unlikely that they will favor repressive laws concerning matters of public decency.

Some may doubt that television and radio should be placed in a "private realm" that is immune from censorship. One obvious point to make is that adults can be their own censors. If a program offends, you can turn it off. But what about children? If parents are concerned about their children being corrupted by radio or television, they can get rid of their radios and televisions. A less drastic solution would be to buy a device that would prevent the radio or television from receiving signals at certain frequencies. In this way, parents could prevent their children from hearing or seeing the programming of certain stations. And they could turn off the device if they wished to hear or see those stations themselves. The market would surely respond to this procedure by providing "family" programming on some stations, while other stations would provide "adult" programs. One point that should be obvious by now is that parents have no right to censor what others can hear or see on radio and television in order to make it easier for them to control what their children can hear or see. Again, this would be a case of restricting the freedom of others in order to promote one's own ends—a clear violation of the freedom principle.

Some persons fear that the abolition of victimless crimes would have dire social consequences. They believe that, if gambling, prostitution, pornography, and the use of illicit drugs are not prohibited, our society will collapse due to moral decay. From a libertarian point of view, this concern about moral decay is ironic because it is the moralists who are acting immorally. They are imposing their values on others, and they are denying others an equal right to be free. Apart from the general concern about "moral decay," there are more specific fears that the abolition of particular victimless crimes will have bad consequences. For example, some persons believe that if heroin is legalized there will be an increase in crime. They argue that heroin users commit many crimes, and if heroin is legalized, there will be more heroin users committing crimes. This argument fails to recognize that many heroin users resort to crime because heroin is very expensive and heroin is costly primarily because it is illegal.[9] However, even if many heroin users would continue to commit crimes after legalization, a libertarian cannot support a general prohibition of heroin use. We should grant each (individual) person an equal right to be free. Suppose that Brown is a heroin user who does not commit crimes to support his habit. If we try to prohibit Brown from using heroin because *other* users commit crimes, we would not respect Brown's basic right.

I hope it is clear that I am not advocating that persons gamble, use dangerous drugs, or go to prostitutes. What is at issue is whether we have the right to punish persons who participate in such activities. If we wish to grant each person an equal right to be free, we must acknowledge that we have no right to punish persons for conduct that does not cause others to behave involuntarily. A libertarian must tolerate many activities, even if he does not (personally) approve of them.

Chapter Four

Property

4.1 My objective in this chapter is to develop a theory of property rights. I shall argue that persons have the right to own things they produce from resources that they have the right to use. This conclusion entails significant limitations on governmental activities. However, I shall also argue that government does have an important role to play in determining who has the right to use which resources.

Let us begin by considering the labor theory of land acquisition. Land can be used for: traveling, hunting, the grazing of domesticated animals, farming, building upon, and aesthetic appreciation. This of course is not a complete list, but is sufficient to establish that land can be used for a variety of purposes. In what circumstances does a person have the right to appropriate land for his own use? One answer is that a person appropriates land by "mixing his labor" with it.[1] Suppose that farmer Brown plows some land and plants a crop. According to the labor theory, Brown is the rightful owner of the land. An embarrassing question for the theory is: What right did Brown have to plow and plant the

57

land in the first place? Suppose, for example, that the land had been used by Smith as grazing land for his sheep. According to the theory, Smith does not own the land because he has not mixed his labor with it. He simply lets his sheep eat the grass, and the grass grows without cultivation. And since Smith has not appropriated the land by mixing his labor with it, the theory entails that farmer Brown does not violate Smith's rights when he appropriates it.

There is a curious agrarian bias within the labor theory; farming is clearly the preferred way of using land. In fact, it is difficult to see how anyone but a farmer can appropriate land. Suppose, for example, that there is one pedestrian path through the mountains. The persons who use this path do not mix their labor with the land; they simply walk on it. Suppose further that a farmer appropriates some of the land that is used for the path by planting a crop. According to the labor theory, this farmer now owns the land, and if he insists, pedestrians should stay off his land.

Suppose that a river gorge is used by persons who enjoy contemplating its scenic beauty. The labor theory entails that these persons do not own the land because they have not mixed their labor with it. In fact, their enjoyment of the land depends on it being left in its natural state. Suppose that a corporation builds a dam in the gorge in order to generate electric power. Since no one owns the land, the corporation does not violate anyone's rights. However, even after the corporation builds the dam, there seems to be no reason to think that the corporation owns the land either. Perhaps it owns the land immediately under the dam; but if it does, an explanation is needed as to why building something *on land* counts as mixing one's labor *with the land*. Furthermore, there is no reason to think that building the dam gives the corporation title to the rest of the gorge. If a farmer could cultivate the land in the gorge, he apparently would become the first owner of the land, and he could prohibit the dam owners from flooding his land.

Let us consider one more case. Suppose that there is a small forest that the Smith family uses as a source of wood; they cut down large trees when they need them. Over the years, the forest regenerates itself. When the large trees are cut down, this creates space for the younger trees to grow. Thus, nature supplies the Smiths with a steady supply of wood. However, according to the labor theory, the Smiths do not own the land. Thus, if a farmer cleared the land, he would not violate the Smiths' rights, and he would become the first owner of the land.

The labor theory of land acquisition is not consistent with the demand of the freedom principle. The theory gives preference to farmers, for it entails that the purposes of farmers are superior to the purposes of non-farmers. As the previous cases demonstrate, the theory does not grant non-farmers an equal right to pursue their ends.

4.2 While the labor theory of land acquisition is unsatisfactory, there are cases in which laboring to produce things does justify the ownership of those things. Suppose that there is an abundance of unowned wood that is available for anyone to gather. Smith gathers some wood, and he uses the wood to make a chair. In this case, Smith would own the chair because he has invested his labor in making it. If another person were to take the chair for his own use, he would violate the freedom principle. By taking the chair without Smith's consent, he would cause Smith to behave involuntarily by forcing Smith to work for him. In other words, since others have a duty not to take the chair, we can conclude that Smith owns it.

The above case illustrates the important rule that persons are entitled to own things they produce from resources that they have the right to use. I understand resources to be things that are valuable for human use that are *not* produced by human beings. Included in the category of resources are land, water, fossil fuels, mineral deposits, plants and trees that grow without cultivation, airwaves for broadcasting, and air-space for travel. Since valuable things like land, mineral deposits, etc. are not produced by human beings, particular individuals have no obvious claim on them. And since these valuable things are typically scarce, civil societies must develop rules for resolving conflicts over who has the right to use which resources. These rules should be consistent with the demand of the freedom principle.

To help us see what the freedom principle requires in this area, I shall introduce some definitions. Let us say that a person is the owner of X when X is his private property. X is a person's private property when (1) the person has exclusive rights of use with respect to X and (2) he can transfer those rights (or any part of them) by gift, bequest, or exchange. A person is the lessee of X when (1) he has exclusive rights of use, but (2) he cannot transfer those rights to others.[2] In this case, X is called leased property. X is public property when everyone has the same rights of use. For example, all persons have the right to use a public park provided they follow the rules (don't shoot guns, don't build fires in the grass, etc.) that apply to all users.

The owners and the lessees of property have exclusive rights of use, but this does not entail that the rights they exercise are unlimited. "A distinction must be drawn between exclusively exercising rights and the range of rights so exercised."[3] For example, the owner of a necktie has the exclusive right to sell it, but he does not have the right (in normal circumstances) to strangle someone with it. The lessee of land may have the exclusive right to build a house on it, but the lease may prohibit him from using the land for commercial purposes.

It should be clear that public property satisfies the demand of the freedom principle. All persons have the same (i.e., equal) rights of use; anyone can use public property as long as he or she follows the rules that apply to all who use it. These rules should not exclude persons due to conditions they cannot help. For example, persons should not be prohibited from using a public beach because they are Jewish, have brown skin, etc. Persons can be excluded on the ground that they are performing acts which are harmful, dangerous, or seriously offensive to others. For example, persons who drive dangerously on public roadways could have their driving license revoked for a period of time. Such restrictions do not take away anyone's rights. Individuals have no right to damage public property, to harm or endanger others, or to do things in public that are seriously offensive to others. To summarize, if individuals choose to refrain from doing what they have no right to do, they will be free to use public property.

A system of property rights in which various resources are leased or owned can satisfy the demand of the freedom principle provided that two conditions are met: (1) all persons have the opportunity to acquire the right to use resources, and (2) those who acquire the exclusive right to use particular resources compensate others for their loss of freedom.

When resources are leased, condition (1) requires that the bidding system be open to all. For instance, persons should not be excluded because of their race, religion, or sex. Condition (1) also requires that the ownership of the most common resource, land, should not be concentrated among a wealthy elite. In certain Latin American countries, this requirement is violated. These countries have feudalistic systems in which huge estates called "latifundios" are owned by wealthy families.[4] In contrast, in the United States land holdings are widely dispersed, and the average working person can afford to own land.

Since the owners and lessees of resources have exclusive rights of use, other persons cannot use the resources unless the owners or lessees give them permission. As a result, the freedom of others is diminished. The owners and lessees should compensate others for their loss of freedom by paying for the right to use the resources. In cases in which resources are leased, there is a simple way of determining compensation. The resources should be leased to the highest bidder, and thus the market would determine the monetary value of the rights to use the resources. The owners of resources can be assessed a resource tax. Ideally, the tax should be equal to what the resource would lease for if it were leased. By following this procedure, owners would compensate others according to the market value of the resource being used.

All citizens have an equal claim on the revenue derived from the leasing of resources and from the resource tax. Thus, the government should distribute this money (minus the administrative costs of regulating the use of resources) in equal shares to all citizens. By following this procedure, all citizens would receive their equal share of the market value of the resources that are being used by private individuals or groups. Money is the appropriate means of compensation because of its neutrality; it can be used, according to one's desire, to purchase property rights in many different things.

4.3 In a society where resources are public, private, or leased property, political decisions must be made concerning the assignment of resources to the different categories. Public property, such as roadways and parks, obviously has important functions. Public roadways allow persons to travel without having to secure the permission of others. Parks provide open areas where persons can relax and participate in recreational activities. However, public property does not satisfy the desire for privacy. For example, there are persons living in houses who would like to prohibit others from using their yards. Apartment dwellers might wish to have a swimming pool for their private use. For various economic reasons, businessmen often would be unwilling to invest in productive enterprises without the security of knowing that they have exclusive rights to use certain resources. Farmers, for example, would like to prohibit others from walking on their plants, picking their crops, etc.

Both leased property and private property can satisfy the desire for privacy. An obvious advantage of leased property is that leasing procedures provide a clear determination of the market value of the resource. In contrast, when the owner of a resource is taxed, assessors must estimate what the resource would lease for *if* it were leased. Since tax assessments can be mistaken, why should we permit the private ownership of resources? Why not lease all resources that are not public property? An obvious disadvantage of this proposal is the huge government bureaucracy that would be required to administer a property system in which most resources are leased. The government would be involved in every exchange of rights to use resources. Such a concentration of power in the hands of politicians would present a serious danger to a free society.

We should also note that the leasing of land presents particular problems because persons often do things on land that increase or decrease the value of the property. For example, suppose that Jones leases some land and builds a house. Jones owns the house, but he does not own the land. Suppose that he wants to move. How can he sell his house? Both the land and the house could be leased to a subsequent lessee. However, Jones should be compensated for his investment in the house, and the government would have to determine what compensation Jones should receive. Suppose that the value of the property has increased in part because the government built a new highway in the area. How can the bureaucrats decide the extent to which the property has increased in value due to Jones's investment?

When Jones moves, suppose that Brown leases the land and the house. Suppose further that Brown allows the house to deteriorate. If Brown were the owner, he would suffer the economic consequences if he subsequently sold the house. But as a lessee, what economic incentive does he have to maintain the house in good condition? Suppose that Brown leases the land and the house for an annual sum of $5000. After ten years, the property is leased to another person for $3000 per year. Should Brown be charged for allowing the value of the property to decrease? Suppose that the property has decreased in value in part because an airport has been built nearby. How can the bureaucrats determine Brown's liability for allowing the condition of the house to deteriorate? These problems suggest that it would be wise (in most cases) not to lease land.

Another advantage of not leasing land is that it would be unnecessary to confiscate land that is now privately owned. Instead, the present owners would simply be assessed a resource tax. If idle land is taxed at its full rate (i.e., the rate that equals what the land would lease for if it were leased), it would have no market value. Only "improved land" would have a selling price; the buyer would be paying for the improvements, not the land. Unowned land can be introduced into the economy by selling it to the highest bidder. The buyer would pay the government a certain sum per year, e.g., $1000. If he sells the property, the new buyer (presumably) would be buying the improvements on the property (e.g., house, yard, orchard, etc.). The new owner would then be assessed a resource tax.

Besides the considerations already mentioned, other values should be taken into account when decisions are made as to whether resources should be public, private, or leased property. One important value is economic productivity. However, this value should be weighed against other values such as the conservation of resources, the control of pollution, and esthetic values. The freedom principle does not tell us which of these values is most important. However, the principle does tell us what the basic structure of the political system (which decides these matters) should be, (see 5.7).

4.4 A free society would have a market economy. This conclusion follows from two rules entailed by the freedom principle: (1) persons have the right to own things they produce from resources that they have the right to use, and (2) persons should not interfere with voluntary economic exchanges.[5] Suppose that Smith is the owner of farm land on which he produces a crop of corn. Since he is the owner of the land, Smith has the right to use it, and he also has the right to own what he produces from the land. If others take what he produces, they would force Smith to work for them, and thus, they would not grant him an equal right to be free, (4.2). Since Smith owns the corn, he has the right to exchange it for other goods or services. In a market economy, voluntary exchanges occur because the parties involved expect to gain from the transactions. When persons interfere with such trades, they deny others an equal right to determine for themselves what their own good is and how to pursue it.

All taxes except the resource tax violate the freedom principle. The resource tax is an exception because the person who pays this tax is paying for the right to use a resource. However, once one acquires the right to use a resource, he is entitled to what he produces from that resource. And since the owners of things have the right to transfer their rights of ownership to others, persons are also entitled to what they acquire from others by gift or exchange. As a result, the government violates the freedom principle when it takes private property by coercive taxation.

One might defend coercive taxation by pointing out that the government provides services in exchange for the property that it takes. However, this is not a voluntary exchange. Those who would prefer to keep their property are threatened with punishment if they fail to pay their taxes. If the exchange were truly voluntary, a person could refuse the services and keep his property. Many (existing) governmental activities are financed by coercive taxation. In a libertarian society, these activities would be financed by voluntary means, or they would be abolished, (see 5.4).

4.5 Let us turn our attention to the problem of conserving resources. Our discussion will be facilitated by introducing some definitions. *Depletable resources* cannot be preserved unless we do not use them. Fossil fuels are examples. *Renewable resources* can regenerate themselves. Examples are trees, fish, and wild animals. *Reclaimable resources* can be used more than once. For example, minerals are used to make various metals which are in turn used in the production of cars, refrigerators, etc. The metals in these products can be recovered and used to make other things. Finally, there are *preservable resources* like air, water, and land. Unlike depletable resources, the use of preservable resources need not lead to their exhaustion, i.e., to a condition in which they can no longer be used.

It is sometimes argued that depletable resources should be preserved for use by future generations. However, if our generation has a duty to preserve depletable resources, then the next generation will presumably have the same duty, and the next generation, etc. In other words, this argument yields the conclusion that depletable resources should never be used by anyone.[6] Others argue that depletable resources should be conserved (rather than preserved). I take their point to be that we should use these resources at a slower rate so that they will last longer. It should be noted that there is a market solution which produces this sort of conservation. As a depletable resource becomes more scarce, its price will rise, and therefore less of it will be used. A higher price will (usually) produce two other benefits: it will encourage persons to use existing substitutes, and it will stimulate the development of new substitutes. If the price of a depletable resource is held below the market price by government controls (as was the case with the price of domestic oil in the United States), future generations are poorly served because the development of substitutes is discouraged.

It has been argued that a generation which exhausts a resource has a duty to develop technologies that will enable the next generation to use various substitutes in place of the depleted resource.[7] One wonders, however, what the present generation must do to satisfy this requirement. For example, imagine that our generation has exhausted the world's oil supplies so that there is no more gasoline for running automobiles and trucks. Suppose that the only available replacement technology involves the use of alcohol as a fuel. Alcohol is made from staple crops like corn, wheat, potatoes, etc. These things are valuable as food as well as being valuable for making fuel. As a result, fuel is scarce, and the next generation has a lower standard of living than we enjoyed. Did we violate our duty to the next generation? Do they have a right to a standard of living at least as high as ours?

Of course, we have no idea what the future will bring. Predictions of impending disaster due to the exhaustion of resources have been made many times in the past, but the disaster never occurred. At one time, persons were concerned about the exhaustion of whale oil, but other persons developed the technology to use oil from the ground instead. And long before fossil fuels are exhausted, persons may develop the technology to use hydrogen as fuel. Or there may be new sources of fuel that are not even being contemplated at this time. New technologies create new resources. For something to be a resource, we must know how to use it. For centuries, oil was not a resource because persons did not know how to use it. In the future, persons will find new resources, i.e., they will discover new ways to tap the hidden potential found in nature.

A strong case can be made for the claim that the ownership of renewable resources provides the best guarantee of their proper management. When a company owns timberland, for example, it has an economic incentive to manage the land so that it will continue to produce wood in the future. Timberland can be farmed. By immediate and careful replanting after harvest, the yield of timberland can be greatly increased. However, for a company to do this, it will usually want the assurance that the profits from growing more trees at a faster rate will not go to someone else. Ownership of the land provides this assurance.

In contrast, if timberland is leased, the lessee has an incentive to harvest as many trees as possible within the period of the lease. And the lessee has no incentive to preserve the capital value of the resource beyond the period of the lease. This example shows why the leasing of renewable resources will usually result in poor management of the resources.

When a renewable resource is public property, there is the danger of what has been called "the tragedy of the commons."[8] In England, sheepherders could graze their animals on public property called the commons.

This policy led to overgrazing because individual herdsmen lacked sufficient incentive to limit the number of their animals. It was in a herdsman's interest to limit his flock only if others did the same; but without such an agreement, economic incentives encouraged the users of the commons to exploit it as rapidly as possible before other users exhausted the resource. If an individual herdsman reduced his flock, that simply left more vegetation for the sheep of other herdsmen.

A similar tragedy occurred in the United States in the nineteenth century. Cattlemen and sheepherders were allowed to graze their animals on western grasslands owned by the federal government. As a result, lush grasslands were destroyed by overgrazing.

> The public domain became stocked with more animals than the range could support. Since each stockman feared that others would beat him to the available forage, he grazed early in the year and did not permit young grass to mature and reseed. Under such conditions, the quality and quantity of available forage rapidly decreased; vigorous perennials gave way to annuals and annuals to weeds.[9]

Overgrazing on public lands set the stage for the "dust bowl" that followed.

One answer to such tragedies is to establish private property rights in renewable resources. When a person owns a renewable resource, he has an economic incentive to preserve the capital value of the resource. When a cattleman owns the grasslands on which his animals forage, for example, he will want to manage the resource so that it will continue to be useful in the future.

In some cases, it would be difficult to establish private property rights in renewable resources. Some fish, like salmon, for example, travel great distances, and thus it would be hard to determine which fish belong to whom. In this kind of case, it may be necessary for the government to manage the resource. The government could lease commercial fishing rights to the highest bidders, and it could insure sustained yields by limiting the number of leases.

Reclaimable resources do not regenerate themselves, but they can be recycled (i.e., used again). As a reclaimable resource becomes scarce (relative to demand), its price will rise. The higher price increases the incentive to recycle the resource. In a market economy, reclaimable resources will be recycled when it is profitable to do so. Intervention by the government is not necessary, and it would result in the inefficient use of resources, labor, and capital, (see 6.2).

Preservable resources can be abused in a number of ways. For example, strip mining may make land unusable as an object of aesthetic contemplation. Air pollution can cause health problems. Pollutants can make water unfit to drink and our water resources unusable for recreational purposes. The standard libertarian response to these abuses is to argue that they will be controlled if private property rights are enforced.[10] I am not persuaded by this argument. While the owners of property usually have an interest in preventing others from polluting their property, the owner himself may abuse the resource. For example, a company may purchase land *because* it wants to use it for strip mining. A business may buy a river *because* it wants to use it as a dumping ground for its wastes, etc. In cases of this sort, property owners can create an environmental mess that future generations will have to deal with.

There has been much debate about whether future generations have rights. It has been argued by some that the idea of future generations having rights does not make sense because nonexistent beings cannot have rights. This is a pseudo-problem. There will be (presumably) future persons, and those persons will have rights. And what we do now (e.g., storing nuclear wastes improperly), can violate their rights. Hence, we have a duty to respect the rights of future persons, and the government can justifiably take steps to protect their rights.

There is another serious problem with the policy of controlling pollution by court enforcement of private property rights. This policy requires that we be able to identify the polluter and his victims. However, I fail to see how, when there are many polluters and pollutees, the courts can decide who is violating the rights of whom.[11] For example, when I drive my car, I pollute the air. But how can any particular individual prove that *my* pollution is affecting him?

The control of pollution is a complex problem. In some cases, political decisions must be made concerning what are acceptable levels of pollution.[12] For example, in order to help control air pollution the government can establish emission standards for automobiles. The justification for this is that each driver is contributing to air pollution which violates the rights of others. However, the government is not obliged to prohibit all violations of the freedom principle, (3.5). For example, a political decision could be made not to prohibit the use of backyard barbecues. When pollution is not legally prohibited, individuals must still make moral decisions about whether to pollute. For example, if my neighbor is bothered by the smell and smoke from my barbecue, perhaps I should not use it on days when the wind is blowing toward his property. Finally, we should note that, when the victims of a polluter are identifiable, they can sue for damages in civil court, (see 5.2). This possibility provides a check on governmental decisions about what are acceptable levels of pollution. When polluters must pay for the damage they cause (in class action suits, for example), this helps to determine the relevant tradeoffs.

Chapter Five

Government

5.1 Some libertarians view government (any government) as the enemy. Historically, we can find ample support for this view since all governments have overstepped their legitimate boundaries. However, there are governmental activities that do not violate the freedom principle. Furthermore, the regulation of the use of resources is one basic governmental activity required by the freedom principle, (4.3). Government must decide whether particular resources will be public property, private property, or leased property. It must establish the rules persons should follow when using public, private, or leased property. It must establish procedures for leasing resources including bidding procedures, payment policies, and the rules for extending or terminating leases. Part of the revenue that the government collects from the leasing of resources and from the resource tax should be distributed in equal shares to all citizens. The remainder should be used to pay the administrative costs of regulating the use of resources. These administrative costs include a number of items that we will now examine.

Our examination will be facilitated by distinguishing between (1) the laws that establish property rules, (2) the administration or execution of these laws, and (3) their enforcement. Laws establishing property rules should be passed by elected political officials, (see 5.7). The salaries of these politicians are included in the administrative costs of regulating the use of resources. Their staffs, office space, and other legitimate expenses must also be paid for. The salaries and offices of government employees who administer these laws constitute an additional expense. Finally, the laws establishing property rules must be enforced. Thus, expenditures for police protection, the criminal court system, and punishment facilities are included in the cost of regulating the use of resources. The cost of national defense is also included since the concern here is to prevent violations of property rules by other countries. To summarize, the cost of regulating the use of resources includes the cost of making, administering, and enforcing the laws which establish property rules.

One might object that when I include law enforcement as part of regulating the use of resources, I am making the unwarranted assumption that all crimes are crimes against property. I would begin my reply to this objection by pointing out that all crimes are committed *somewhere.* The robber, for example, who attacks his victim in a public park violates the rules concerning proper use of the park. The murderer who lures his victim into his house violates the rules governing the use of private property. Rules prohibiting the use of property for purposes of robbery or murder do not violate the rights of potential offenders because they have no right to rob or murder other persons. Thus, I am not claiming that all crimes are crimes against property in the sense that there are no human victims. Instead, criminal use of property is prohibited *because* we want to prevent victimizations.

The government must decide what sort of currency it will accept in payment for leases and for the resource tax. I assume that the government will issue currency and that lease and tax payments will be made in this currency. However, legal tender laws which prohibit private citizens from agreeing to exchanges involving the use of other currencies or coins violate the freedom principle. In other words, the government has no right to prohibit voluntary exchanges involving the use of other currencies and coins by claiming a monopoly over the issue of currency. For example, persons should be allowed to own gold coins and make payments to other individuals in gold coins. Persons should also be allowed to enter into contracts that call for payments in other national currencies.[1]

5.2 Governmental activities involving regulation of the use of resources should be paid for by revenue derived from the leasing of resources and from the resource tax. Since all taxes except the resource tax violate the freedom principle (4.6), other governmental activities that cannot be financed by noncoercive means should be terminated. However, there are a number of services that the government could provide without resorting to the use of coercive taxation.

The government could establish a civil court system. Unlike a criminal court which determines whether the accused should be punished, a civil court settles disputes between persons. For example, Smith might sue Jones for injury or damage caused by the latter. If Smith wins, Jones would be required to pay compensation. A civil court could also settle disputes over the fulfillment of contracts. One important difference between civil and criminal proceedings is that, before punishment is meted out, the criminal court must establish that the offender should *not* be excused. In contrast, a civil court need not concern itself with excusing conditions. When the tort-feasor (for example) is required to compensate his victim, the assumption is that, since a loss has been caused, it is the tort-feasor who should suffer the loss. Thus, the tort-feasor can be required to make the victim "whole again." Whether the loss was caused intentionally or not is irrelevant.[2]

In tort cases, there must be a violation of the freedom principle which means that (as a necessary condition) one person must cause another person to behave involuntarily. For instance, a boxer who voluntarily participates in a prize fight cannot sue his opponent if he is injured. In contrast, when Jones causes an automobile accident by driving into Smith's car, Jones causes Smith to behave involuntarily. Smith could sue to obtain compensation for injury or damage caused by Jones. When Jones is ordered to pay compensation, this coercion is justified on the ground of self-defense. Smith seeks to reestablish that condition of equality between himself and Jones which existed before Jones caused him to behave involuntarily. In practice, this may be impossible (some losses are not compensable), but in theory at least the end sought is for Jones to make Smith whole again.

There are a number of ways to pay for a civil court system. Parties who wish to have their contracts enforced by the government could be charged a contract fee.[3] Those who do not wish to avail themselves of this service could trust each other, or they could agree to take any disputes that might arise to a private arbitrator. Hence, the voluntary nature of the contract fee is preserved; those who wish to receive the service are simply required to pay for it. Persons who wish to have the right to use the civil court system in tort cases could be charged a "membership" fee along with annual "dues" to keep their membership active. Another possibility would be to allow a nonmember to have his case heard if he posts a bond covering the expected costs of the legal proceedings. The nonmember would bear the court costs whether he wins or loses his case, but he may expect to win a large enough settlement to make the expenditure of time and money financially worthwhile.

The quasi-legal service known as certification could be offered by the government. We have already noted that licensure, insofar as it prohibits voluntary exchanges, violates the freedom principle, (2.3). Instead of licensure, the government could certify that doctors, lawyers, accountants, restaurants, etc. have met certain specified standards. For example, the conditions in which food is stored and prepared in restaurants could be inspected and certified as sanitary by an agency of the government. If customers prefer to go to certified establishments, it will be financially advantageous for restaurant owners to seek certification. And the owners should pay the administrative costs of the certification program. If the individuals and businesses who wish to be certified are unwilling to bear the costs, then there should be no certification programs.

5.3 When it is technically efficient to have a single producer or enterprise, we have what Milton Friedman calls a technical monopoly.[4] For example, it is inefficient for a community to have more than one supplier of water or sewer services because it is inefficient for competing firms to lay more than one set of pipes. There are three ways to deal with a technical monopoly: (1) private firms can supply the service and set their own prices; (2) government can regulate the prices charged by private firms; or (3) government can supply the service. The freedom principle does not tell us which alternative to choose. However, if government does supply the service, it should not use revenue derived from coercive taxes to pay for the cost of the service. Instead, the users of the service should be charged a fee that will adequately cover the cost.

Similar observations apply to the operation of roads; users should pay for construction and maintenance. On limited access roads, like the major turnpikes, it is easy to identify the users by means of tollgates. However, it would not be practical to establish tollgates on each city street. Still there are various ways to identify and charge the users of streets that are not toll roads. For example, the owners of vehicles could be charged a license fee, and they could be assessed further fees depending on the weight of their vehicle and how many miles it is driven. Drivers could keep their receipts for fees paid while using toll roads, and these fees could be subtracted from their "mileage" fee.

The construction and maintenance of parks should also be paid for by those who use the parks. Where there is limited access, this can be done by charging an entrance fee. In other cases, the users of parks could be required to purchase a "park permit." Such a procedure would be similar to the common practice of requiring hunters and fishermen to purchase a license. Seeking voluntary contributions is still another possibility. Those who value using parks would probably contribute to a voluntary payment scheme.

5.4 There are three morally permissible ways for government to acquire the revenue to pay for its activities: (1) the cost of regulating the use of resources can be paid for by revenue from the leasing of resources and from the resource tax; (2) government services can be paid for by those who use the services; and (3) government programs can be financed by voluntary contributions. Many existing government programs are financed by morally impermissible means. These programs authorize the compulsory transfer of wealth from some individuals to others. An example is the parity price support program for agricultural products. This program insures that certain farmers receive a specified price for their products regardless of market conditions. Other examples include foreign aid and various welfare programs such as aid to families with dependent children, public housing, food stamps, and medicaid. If these programs cannot be financed by voluntary contributions, they should be abolished.

No doubt many supporters of these programs are well-intentioned. However, when they insist on financing these programs by coercive taxation, they are supporting the seizure of money that rightfully belongs to other persons. The do-gooders who compel others to support their worthy causes are acting as if *their* ends were superior to the ends of others, (see 7.4). They do not grant other persons an equal right to be free.

Some government programs should be abolished because they are financed by coercive taxes; others should be abolished because they prohibit voluntary exchanges. The various measures restricting foreign trade are clear examples. Suppose that Smith wishes to purchase a shipment of

Italian shoes from Cardoza, but the government prohibits the purchase because it exceeds the import quota for Italian shoes. Supporters of the quota claim that domestic shoe manufacturers should be protected. In other words, they are assuming that their end (the protection of domestic shoe manufacturers) is superior to the ends of Smith and Cardoza. Such interference with voluntary exchanges obviously violates the freedom principle.

Minimum wage laws should also be abolished. Suppose that I wish to work for Jones at $2.00 per hour. However, the government prohibits this exchange by requiring that employers pay $3.00 per hour. If I am lucky, Jones will hire me at $3.00 per hour. If not, we will both be the victims of government interference.

Governments also interfere with freedom of contract by granting special privileges to labor unions. In the United States, labor monopolies have been created by requiring companies to bargain with unions that win a majority vote of the members of a work unit as defined by the government. If a union wins a representation election, it becomes the bargaining agent for all employees in the work unit, and all employees must join the union (whether they support it or not). The company is then required to bargain "in good faith" with the union. Compulsory collective bargaining violates the right of employers to use their own capital. The "union shop" laws also interfere with the freedom of workers; no employee should be compelled to join a union in order to keep his job.[5] The economic effects of these policies will be discussed in the next chapter, (6.2).

5.5   Since public schools are financed by coercive taxes, there would be no public schools in a free society. How would parents (or legal guardians) pay for their children's schooling? The first thing to note is that, since there would be no compulsory schooling laws in a free society, all parents would have the option of educating their children at home. Secondly, since the tax burden would be much lower, parents would have more money to spend for many purposes, including paying tuition. We should also note that all citizens, including children, will receive an equal share of the revenue from the leasing of resources and from the resource tax. For paternalistic reasons, these payments would go to the parents of young children (rather than to the children directly), and the money could be used for tuition. Finally, we can expect that there would be scholarship assistance to the children of needy families. Many private schools offer scholarships now, and scholarship programs could be expanded. Persons are usually quite generous in their support of worthy causes, and in a libertarian society, they would have more money to give to needy children.

The government could play a role in providing financial assistance to older students.[6] Loans could be offered to students who are old enough to assume the requisite responsibility. The government could sell bonds to acquire the initial capital for a student loan program, and payment schedules should be set so that the program would be self-financing. Since student loans are offered by private institutions, why should the government provide this service? It is doubtful that private institutions would make loans to the more needy students. An eighteen-year-old college student, for example, will usually lack the collateral necessary to secure a conventional loan. His parents might be willing to be co-signers, but not all parents would be willing (or able) to accept this sort of obligation. Since student loans are risky, banks would probably charge high interest rates, and this in turn would increase the likelihood of default. The federal government, in contrast, could virtually insure that loan recipients would pay off their loans. If a loan recipient fails to make his payments, the government can withhold his equal share of the revenue derived from the leasing of resources and from the resource tax.

5.6 Would a free society be a just society? If we believe that in a just society goods must be distributed according to some pattern, then a free society would not be a just society. As Robert Nozick has pointed out, liberty upsets patterns.[7] To cite a simple example, suppose a government believes that income should be distributed according to need. Furthermore, this government assumes that all adults have equal needs, unless they have special handicaps such as blindness or deafness, in which case they have greater needs and they receive a larger income. Suppose that the state controls all jobs, and all adults who are able are required to work. Mary is a janitor. She is not handicapped, so she is paid the same salary as most workers. Mary is also an artist, and she paints in her spare time. She sells her paintings to friends and acquaintances, and as a result of these voluntary exchanges, her income is greater than that of other nonhandicapped workers. If the government is serious about enforcing its patterned conception of justice, this sort of creeping capitalism must be prohibited.

In a free society, the distribution of goods will not fit any preconceived pattern.

> The set of holdings that results when some persons receive their marginal products, others win at gambling, others receive a share of their mate's income, others receive gifts from foundations, others receive interest on loans, others receive gifts from admirers, others receive returns on investment, others make for themselves much of what they have, others find things, and so on, will not be patterned.[8]

Instead of a patterned conception, the freedom principle entails an historical conception of justice. Persons are entitled to the holdings they acquire as long as they do not violate the rights of others. Suppose that Jones earns $100,000 in one year, while Brown earns $10,000. Is this just? According to the freedom principle, the answer depends on how this distribution came about. Suppose that Jones is a popular rock singer who earns $100,000 by giving a concert. Brown is a folk singer who earns $10,000 by working in coffee houses on weekends. Both acquire their income by voluntary exchanges, no rights are violated, and the distribution is just.

Can a theory that ignores people's needs be the correct theory of justice? To answer this question, we must examine the concept of need. In one sense of 'need,' a person needs whatever is necessary for him to do what he wants to do. If I want to go fly fishing, for example, then I will need (among other things) an appropriate pole. If I want to see the ballet, I will need a ticket. My needs vary with my different wants. If I no longer want to go fly fishing, I will no longer need a pole. I assume that no credible theory of justice entails that everyone's variable and subjective needs should be satisfied. The jet-set playboy may need his own jet in order to carry out his plans, but surely justice does not require that such an extravagance be provided.

Are there objective needs, i.e., needs that all persons have regardless of their variable wants? A "yes" answer can be argued for by noting that, whatever a person wants to do, he must be alive to do it, and human beings need air, water, food, clothing, and shelter to survive. On the other hand, it can be argued that all needs are dependent upon, and thus relative to, wants. In the case of "objective needs," these needs are generated by the desire to continue to live. Only persons who want to continue to live have a need for the basic necessities of life, and persons can (and sometimes do) choose not to continue to live. Patrick Henry's famous preference, "Give me liberty or give me death," illustrates this point. However, for the sake of argument, let us ignore this complication and assume that all persons do have objective needs.

Let us examine the claim that the objective needs of all citizens should be met. One of the problems with this claim is that there are cases in which persons have an objective need for medical care. If a person has a shortened life expectancy due to a medical problem, then his survival (at some point) depends on the receipt of medical treatment. Suppose that Jones is a quadriplegic who has a shortened life expectancy due to his inability to participate in normal exercise. While there is nothing that we can do for Jones at this time, perhaps something could be done if enough time and money were invested in research. Perhaps researchers could develop "bionic" arms and legs which would allow Jones to exercise "normally." Suppose that this research would cost $10 billion. Does Jones have a right to this medical treatment? Who has the duty to pay for it? These questions are not fanciful, for unlimited amounts of money could be spent on medical research. I assume however, that no society will devote most of its wealth and energies to medical research. Hence, if medical care is recognized as being an objective need, it is difficult to know what is being claimed when one says that the objective needs of all citizens should be met. Since this is a problem primarily for those who hold that we have extensive positive duties to help others, I shall set it aside and return to my original assumption that air, water, food, shelter, and clothing are objective needs.

Let us now compare the following claims:

(1) The objective needs of all citizens should be met.
(2) Government should insure that the objective needs of all citizens are met.

The first thing to note is that these are *distinct* claims; a person can accept (1) without accepting (2). One might believe, for example, that programs to help the needy should be administered by private charities because governmental programs are ill-conceived and poorly managed, (see 6.5). If (2) requires that the government raise revenue by means of coercive taxes, the libertarian will obviously reject it. What is the libertarian position on (1)? Libertarians hold that helping the needy is the proper province of charity unless special circumstances pertain, (1.4). In most cases, we have no duty to help, and the government has no right to make such assistance compulsory. However, libertarians can accept (1) in the sense in which it is understood as a *recommendation* that the needy by helped, i.e., it would be a good thing if the objective needs of all citizens were met. Furthermore, I firmly believe that the objective needs (narrowly defined) of all citizens would be met in a libertarian society. There is ample evidence that persons are generous in their support of worthy causes. In 1978, for example, Americans contributed $39.56 billion to charities as well as educational and cultural institutions.[9]

Is a free society a just society? We have noted that the freedom principle entails an historical conception of justice—distributions of burdens and benefits are just so long as no one's rights have been violated. Assuming that there are good reasons for accepting the freedom principle, the free society is a just society. Even if this is granted, one might still object that a libertarian society is unattractive because it lacks compassion. However, there is nothing noble about supporting worthy causes because one is compelled to do so. Genuine benevolence exists only when we freely give of our time and money.

5.7   From a libertarian point of view, there are severe moral limits on what government can do. However, the government in a free society would still have important functions, most notably those associated with regulating the use of resources. Governmental policies in this area would have a significant impact on the freedom of each citizen; therefore all citizens should have an equal right to participate in their formulation. This equal right of participation entails that the opportunity to seek political office should be open to all. Furthermore, all citizens should have the opportunity to participate directly in the process that determines who has political authority. This means that political offices must be elective, with the vote of each citizen counting equally. Finally, all citizens should have the right to express their political opinions and the concomitant right to join with others in pursuit of their political ideals.

Because people differ in many ways, the equal right of participation does not guarantee that each citizen will have the same political power or influence, (1.5). For example, those who have a special talent for articulating political beliefs can make more effective use of the right to express their political opinions. Few persons (in the United States at least) have advocated that talented thinkers and writers be restrained from expressing their political views. However, a very similar restriction is advocated by many persons, i.e., that campaign contributions which exceed a specified amount be prohibited. This prohibition violates the affected persons' right of participation. If I am prohibited from giving my money to a spokesman for causes that I believe in, then it is *my* freedom of speech and *my* right to join with others in pursuit of political ideals which are violated. Many persons also advocate the practice of using public monies to finance the campaigns of politicians in the major political parties. The supposed rationale for this "reform" is to help equalize political influence.[10] In fact, this program helps the dominant political parties, and thus it increases the power of those who already have the most political power. What is even worse from a libertarian point of view is that it compels persons (by means of coercive taxation) to support political ideas and causes they oppose. When politicians require contributions to their campaigns, they do not grant others an equal right to be free.

Democracy is best understood as a political process in which citizens enjoy the equal right of participation. Thus, a democracy differs from a dictatorship because it has open and free elections, all citizens can run for political office, all citizens can express their political opinions, etc. In a *constitutional* democracy, certain matters are placed outside the scope of the political process. For example, in the United States freedom of religion is guaranteed by the Constitution, and thus the majority cannot vote to limit the religious freedom of a minority. A libertarian society would have a constitutional democracy. Individuals have rights, and these rights should not be violated by political decisions. For example, the constitution should specify that all taxes, except the resource tax, are prohibited. It should guarantee the right of adults to participate in voluntary economic exchanges, and so on. I shall say more about this topic in the next chapter, (6.5).

5.8 We have noted that the provision of national defense is a legitimate governmental function, (5.1). The objective of governmental policies in this area should be to defend the country from foreign aggression. The objective is not to police the world. Thus, a government should not take money from its citizens in order to finance its foreign adventures. Suppose that North Korea attacks South Korea. Would the American government be justified in sending military aid to South Korea? Individual American citizens would have the right to send aid—but not the government. Helping South Korea is not a moral requirement (1.4), and thus government officials have no right to make this commitment for others. Governments should pursue a noninterventionist foreign policy. For the United States, a policy of nonintervention would require that the government end its involvement in military alliances with other regimes. Foreign aid programs should be abolished, foreign bases dismantled, and American troops stationed in other countries should be brought home.

Wouldn't the withdrawal of the American military presence in other countries lead to aggression by the Soviet Union? This is possible, but the American government has no right to compel American taxpayers to pay for the defense of other countries. Furthermore, the American experience in Viet-Nam and the Soviet experience in Afghanistan demonstrate that it is difficult to conquer even a small, technologically backward country. History demonstrates that an imperialistic foreign policy is very expensive. The Soviet Union, which has a corrupt political system and an inefficient economy, has more than enough problems trying to maintain its present empire.

When one indulges in pure speculation, one can imagine a situation in which Soviet aggression against another country would endanger American security. Suppose that the Soviet Union launches an attack with troops and conventional weapons against Canada. Soviet control of Canada would certainly threaten American security. Hence, for reasons of national defense, the American government could help the Canadians repel such an attack. But again, as long as the American government (and the Canadian government) maintain adequate defenses, such an attack would be suicidal for the Soviets.

If the American government pursued a purely defensive military strategy, this would result in an immediate and dramatic reduction in the size of the military budget. Our present manpower requirements are based on the assumption that American military forces must be prepared to fight simultaneous wars in Europe and Asia. Once this assumption is dropped, the arguments for the military draft lose what little plausibility they might have. Libertarians of course oppose any military draft. Conscription into the armed forces is involuntary servitude (i.e., slavery). The military should hire employees like any other governmental agency. If it is necessary to pay high salaries in order to attract competent employees, then the military should pay high salaries. When the government hires police, it offers monetary compensation sufficient to attract competent personnel. There is no reason to treat military employees differently.

Are there limits to the right of a country to defend itself? In particular, given that the use of modern weapons will result in the deaths of innocent persons, does a country have the right to use modern weapons? Since the freedom principle applies to (individual) persons, we must ask whether individuals have the right to kill innocent persons in the process of defending themselves. I assume that the word 'innocent' refers to the *moral* innocence of the victims, and thus a person who is not morally responsible for his wrongdoing is (morally) innocent. Suppose that a mentally deranged person attacks Smith with a knife, and Smith defends himself by shooting and killing the person. Furthermore, Smith must kill this person in order to save his own life. In this case, Smith has the right to kill his attacker even though the person is innocent, i.e., not morally responsible for his action. Smith does not assume that he has a superior right to be free; instead he defends his equal right to be free by preventing a relationship in which he would have been treated as if he were inferior.

Suppose that Jones is shooting at Smith. Smith is temporarily protected by a wooden barrier, but it is being destroyed by Jones's bullets. Smith also has a gun, but Jones is protected by an innocent hostage that he is using as a shield. Smith can kill Jones and save his own life only if he first kills the hostage.[11] If Smith has the right to kill his deranged attacker in the first case, consistency requires that we grant him the right to kill the innocent hostage in the second case. We must conclude that defenders have the right to kill innocent persons when the killing is necessary to save their own lives.

When a country defends itself by using modern weapons, innocent persons will be killed. This is morally permissible so long as the killing of innocent persons is necessary to defend the lives of the persons who are being attacked. However, this qualification exposes the pointlessness of nuclear war. If the Soviet Union, for example, launches a nuclear attack against the United States and the United States responds with a nuclear counterattack, the destruction will be so great that any survivors may wish that they had been victims. The massive destructive power of modern weapons makes mutual disarmament an urgent necessity. If the United States were to pursue a noninterventionist foreign policy, this would help to create a climate of opinion favorable to mutual disarmament.

Libertarians who are anarchists have difficulty with the problem of aggression by other countries. As David Friedman acknowledges, it is "the hard problem."[12] There is a possible response to this problem that parallels the anarchistic "solution" to the need for protection against criminals. Anarchists assume that most persons would be protected from criminals by private protection agencies. Likewise, private organizations could acquire weapons to defend themselves and their property from foreign aggression. In the United States, for example, there are a number of anti-communist groups who would be likely candidates to fill the national defense void created by the demise of government. Groups like the John Birch Society, the Minutemen, and the Ku Klux Klan come immediately to mind. These groups could acquire their own nuclear weapons, and they could threaten retaliation against any foreign aggressor. There are a number of problems with this anarchist "solution." For one thing, it would make the negotiation of mutual disarmament virtually impossible. The extremists who are attracted to groups like the Minutemen are unlikely to be interested in disarmament. Furthermore, there would be no government to control these groups and insure that their weapons are used for defensive purposes. For instance, suppose that the John Birch Society objects to the actions of Cuban troops in Africa. In an anarchistic society, there would be no government to prevent them from launching a nuclear attack against the Cuban troops. The specter of the John Birch Society controlling submarines armed with nuclear weapons is hardly reassuring.

Chapter Six

Utopia

6.1 According to a common view, the utopian thinker is an impractical dreamer. This view is expressed in one of the definitions for the word 'utopian' given by *The Shorter Oxford English Dictionary:* "Impracticably ideal; of impossible and visionary perfection, especially in respect of politics, social organizations, etc." Is the vision of a society based on the freedom principle utopian (in the above sense)? To answer this question, let us look at two different interpretations of the charge that the free society is impracticable.

First, a critic might point out that most persons do not share my libertarian views, and thus the outlook is not good for the radical changes I have proposed. However, since I believe there are good reasons for accepting the freedom principle, I must also believe that others can be persuaded to adopt the libertarian point of view. In the meantime, the ideal of a free society can serve a practical function. Practical proposals can be judged on the basis of whether their implementation will move society away from or toward the ideal of human freedom. For example, libertarians favor the legalization of marijuana. In the United States today, the forces opposed to the use of marijuana can easily block any effort to legalize it. However libertarians can support the decriminalization of marijuana, i.e., making the possession of small amounts a misdemeanor instead of a felony. Decriminalization is not the ideal, but it would result in less users being sent to prison. It moves us toward the ideal.

The second charge of impracticability is more sweeping. According to this version, even if a majority wished to establish a free society, there is no way to get from here to there. In other words, it would not be possible to make the necessary changes. In order to demonstrate that this charge is false, I will offer some proposals that would facilitate the transition to a free society. I will focus on three major governmental activities and make suggestions as to appropriate changes.

We have noted that social security programs which compel workers to save for their retirement should be abolished, (2.3). How can this be done? A first step would be to stop enrolling new workers in the program. Those who are already participating could be offered the option of terminating their involvement. A formula could be devised to insure them the benefits that they (and their employers) have already paid for. Those present participants who choose to continue in the program would also receive the benefits to which their payments entitle them. Due to the fiscal unsoundness of the social security program in the United States, future benefits would have to be paid for by coercive taxes. This is unfortunate, but there are moral as well as practical reasons for continuing coercive taxation during the transition to a free society. Persons have made plans based on expectations created by the present social security program. They have taken certain courses of action based on these expectations, and the sudden abolition of social security would be the cause of involuntary behavior, i.e., they would not have made this or that choice if they had known that the program would be abolished.

How can government extricate itself from the operation of public schools? One answer is to begin by giving tuition vouchers to parents who prefer to send their school-age children to private schools. Given the quality of public schools in the United States, many parents would choose this option. As enrollments in public schools decline, some of the property previously used for this purpose could be leased or sold to those who wish to establish private schools. Eventually, the direct funding of public schools would end; all schools would charge tuition or find some other nongovernmental means of support. Finally, the tuition voucher program would be abolished. With lower taxes, parents would have more money to use for the education of their children. Also, all citizens, including children, would receive an equal share of the revenue from the leasing of resources and from the resource tax. This money could be used to help pay tuition, (5.5).

How can welfare programs be abolished? The first step would be to announce dates for the termination of particular programs. Again, persons have made choices based on expectations created by these programs, and unless they are given time to make new plans, the sudden demise of welfare could result in a variety of involuntary choices. A second step would be to substitute cash payments to the needy as other welfare programs are abolished. Finally, these cash payments can be replaced by the payments that all citizens receive as their equal share of the revenue from the leasing of resources and from the resource tax. I am not assuming that these payments will be sufficient in every case to meet the needs of those who were previously on welfare. Instead, I assume that private charities will provide aid to those who need it. However, due to improvements in the economy, there should be fewer persons who need help, (see 6.2 and 6.5).

I have neither the time nor the knowledge to set forth an outline of every necessary change. Hopefully, my suggestions have shown that conservatives are wrong to think that major changes cannot be made. If we have the will, change is possible. We are not locked into the present system; there are practical ways to make the changes necessary to bring about a free society.

6.2 Let us say that utopia is the best *possible* society. It is of course my contention that a free society, a society based on the freedom principle, is utopia. Not only is a free society morally right, it is also the best society in terms of two other important social values—economic productivity and social cooperation. Hence, there is a happy coincidence of the Right and the Good. To see this let us examine how a free market economy operates.

A market economy is characterized by cooperation. When Smith and Jones participate in a voluntary economic exchange, they do so because each one expects to gain from it. Their cooperation is based on mutual self-interest. In a modern economy, there is extensive division of labor; most workers perform a specialized task. As a result, there is mutual interdependence. The doctor depends on the farmer to grow food, the farmer depends on the doctor for medical treatment, and they both depend on the shoemaker for shoes, etc. This cooperation also leads to greater productivity since it allows individuals to utilize their special skills in producing particular goods and services.

The free market provides businessmen with an incentive to invest their energies and capital in the production of goods and services. The incentive is profit. So long as the businessman provides a good or a service that commands a market value in excess of his costs of production, he has an incentive to continue his investment. To make a profit, the businessman must produce goods and services efficiently. Those who cannot meet this test are driven out of the market. Thus, the tendency of markets is to place the factors of production (labor, resources, and capital) in the hands of the most efficient producers, and this leads to increased productivity.[1]

When the government interferes with the operation of free markets, the result is lower productivity.[2] Suppose, for example, that the government intervenes in order to save Business X by giving it a subsidy. In support of this policy, it is argued that unless the government intervenes jobs will be lost, workers will be forced onto the welfare roles, and the whole economy will suffer. What this special pleading ignores is that the taxpayers who pay for this subsidy lose as much as Business X gains. Consumers will have less income to spend on other things, and thus other industries will be hurt because of the subsidy to Business X. Furthermore, in a growing economy, it is necessary that inefficient businesses die. The factors of production are limited, and inefficient businesses use labor, capital, and resources that should be released for growing businesses. When the government intervenes to save businesses, it insures that labor, capital, and resources will be used by less efficient producers, and the average standard of living will be lower as a result.[3]

The demand for tariffs is another form of special pleading. The obvious result of tariffs is that consumers must pay more for the affected goods; thus, they have less money to spend on other goods and services. What the protected industry gains, other industries lose. Still the cry of "save American jobs" is often persuasive. However, this "justification" is based on a fundamental misunderstanding of how markets operate. The effects of tariffs can be seen by examining the most extreme case. Suppose that tariff barriers are raised so high that it is unprofitable to sell any foreign goods in the United States. Industries that were competing with foreign businesses will be helped by this policy; they can raise their prices. Consumers will obviously be hurt, but the damage to the economy will be much more extensive than this. Since Americans will not be buying foreign goods, foreigners will not have dollars to buy American goods. Hence, industries that previously sold goods to other nations will have to cut back on production and lay off workers. These workers may find employment in the industries that are helped by tariffs. However, the American standard of living will decrease because capital, resources, and labor will be used less efficiently; we will be producing things that can be produced (comparatively speaking) more efficiently in other countries. If tariffs keep out some goods (and not all goods), the effects will be the same only less severe.

Whether or not one of two regions is absolutely more efficient in the production of every good than is the other, if each specializes in the products in which it has a *comparative advantage* (greatest *relative* efficiency), trade will be mutually profitable to both regions. Real wages of productive factors will rise in both places. An ill-designed prohibitive tariff, far from helping the protected factor of production, will instead reduce its real wage by making imports expensive and by making the whole world less productive through eliminating the efficiency inherent in the best pattern of specialization and division of labor.[4]

Economists have known since the time of Adam Smith (at least) that foreign trade is beneficial, but still the special pleading continues.

Government intervention in the form of tariffs leads to higher prices for the affected goods. Government can also interfere with the operation of a free market by trying to lower prices. For example, suppose that consumers complain that the price of eggs is too high because chicken farmers are making exorbitant profits. If the profits of egg producers are higher than the profits of other businesses, it is because the demand for eggs exceeds the supply. If the market is left alone, this situation will be corrected. The high profits in the egg industry will attract new suppliers. As the supply of eggs increases, the price will fall. If the government controls the price of eggs at a level below the market price, the result will be chronic shortages. There will be persons who would prefer to spend their money on eggs who will be denied the opportunity because there are no eggs to buy. There will be persons who would be willing (in the absence of price controls) to produce eggs but will not do so because they can invest their energies and capital more profitably elsewhere. In a market economy, prices must be allowed to change so that businesses can respond to changes in supply and demand. When the government interferes with the prices of goods, it insures that labor, resources, and capital will be misallocated. When the price of a good is set higher than the market price, production is encouraged while consumption is discouraged. The result is overproduction. Surpluses caused by the parity price support program for agricultural products are classic examples. When the price of a good is set below the market price, production is discouraged and consumption is encouraged. As a result, not enough is produced. An example would be a shortage of housing caused by the imposition of rent controls.

When the government interferes with the market price of labor, the result, once again, is a misallocation of labor, resources, and capital. One illustration is the unemployment caused by minimum wage laws. Some workers, particularly the young and inexperienced, are not very productive, and legislating a minimum wage will not change this fact. When the minimum wage is set at a rate higher than the market price some workers are able to command for their labor, they will not find employment. And society is deprived of their productive capacities, as modest as they may be. Much worse is the fact that many teenagers are denied entry into the job market, thereby failing to acquire the skills that would prepare them to find better paying jobs.[5]

In some cases, the price of labor is determined by bargaining between management and union monopolies. Is this helpful to workers? No doubt some employees benefit from this arrangement, for their unions negotiate higher wages than they would receive in a free market. However, as Milton Friedman points out, less than one quarter of the workers in the United States are unionized. Furthermore, many unions are weak, and they have little influence on the wage rates of their members.[6] For purposes of illustration let us assume that ten percent of American workers belong to strong unions and that these unions are able to secure wage agreements in excess of what their members could command in a free market. As a result, fewer workers are employed in these industries, which means that more workers must seek employment in other sectors of the economy, and wages are lower in the other sectors.

If unions raise wage rates in a particular occupation or industry, they necessarily make the amount of employment available in that occupation or industry less than it otherwise would be—just as any higher price cuts down the amount purchased. The effect is an increased number of persons seeking other jobs, which forces down wages in other occupations. Since unions have generally been strongest among groups that would have been high-paid anyway, their effect has been to make high-paid workers higher paid at the expense of lower-paid workers. Unions have therefore not only harmed the public at large and workers as a whole by distorting the use of labor; they have also made the incomes of the working class more unequal by reducing the opportunities available to the most disadvantaged workers.[7]

The myth of labor solidarity is a cruel hoax. The high wages that the members of strong unions receive harm the majority of workers.

There are two general responses that businesses can make when unions secure wage rates above the free market price for labor. In some circumstances, a business can pass the cost on to the consumer by raising the price of its goods or services. In this case, sales will decrease, and the business will employ less workers. When a business cannot raise the price of its goods or services, the higher cost of labor will come out of its profits. If the profit margin falls below the return that investors can receive elsewhere, investment in the business will decline. Lack of investment will lead eventually to less employment. A business can absorb a higher than market price for labor without loss of employment only in the case in which it is making high profits *relative to other companies.* This case, needless to say, must be the exception.

In a market economy, there is no natural antagonism between workers and employers. The businessman needs the worker, and the worker needs the businessman. They both expect to gain from their voluntary exchange, which is why they agree to interact. Likewise, since they are consumers, they both benefit from economic arrangements that increase production and raise their standard of living. And since a free market is the most productive economic system, they both benefit from a market economy.

In contrast, governmental intervention in the economy leads to social conflict as various interest groups press their demands for special treatment. Persons worry about how the "economic pie" will be divided, and as governmental intervention leads to lower productivity, this concern intensifies. When the government caters to the special interest of one group, the demand for special treatment is taken up by more and more groups. Every group wants its special tariff, subsidy, tax exemption, etc. But each granting of favors causes misallocation of labor, capital, and resources. Social antogonism increases as each group blames other groups for its economic distress. And they demand that government solve their problems through further governmental intervention. This unhappy scenario is being played out in more and more countries. It is time to reverse the trend.

6.3   No defense of free markets would be complete without examining the issue of business monopolies.[8] The most obvious business monopolies in the United States have been created by governmental intervention. The government, for example, has prohibited price competition in the interstate trucking industry by fixing the rates that truckers can charge; the post office has a monopoly on the delivery of first class mail because the government prohibits competition, etc. In a free society these monopoly arrangements would be abolished.[9]

The critics of free markets are hard pressed to produce actual examples of private monopolies. The American auto industry, which is dominated by General Motors, is sometimes cited as an example. However, there are at least fifteen major manufacturers of automobiles in the world. In a free society, there would be no tariffs on imported cars, and the American market would be highly competitive. Given the lack of actual private monopolies, the critics resort to theories—they theorize that monopolies will develop. However, even if a monopoly did develop, it would have to behave as if it had competitors, for there will always be potential competitors. The case of Alcoa Aluminum is instructive. In a famous antitrust case, Alcoa was accused of conspiring to keep out competitors by steadily lowering its prices and increasing production. Judge Learned Hand wrote the majority opinion:

> It was not inevitable that (Alcoa) should always anticipate increases in the demand for ingot and be prepared to supply them. Nothing compelled it to keep doubling and redoubling its capacity before others entered the field. It insists that it never excluded competitors; but we can think of no more effective exclusion than progressively to embrace each new opportunity as it opened, and to face every newcomer with new capacity already geared into a great organization, having the advantage of experience, trade connection

and the elite of personnel.[10]

Suppose that Alcoa had behaved differently. Instead of passing the lower costs of production on to the customer, suppose it sought larger profits by keeping the price steady, or even raising the price. This would have encouraged other firms to enter the market. But even before competitors appeared, Alcoa would lose sales as its former customers turned to substitutes for aluminum. A higher price for aluminum will lead to greater use of steel, plastic, wood, etc. The free market makes it very difficult for firms to "misbehave."

6.4 Some critics object to market economies precisely because they are so productive. According to these critics, societies that have free markets become too preoccupied with materialistic concerns, and the artistic, intellectual, and spiritual side of man is neglected. However, in a free society, those who wish to pursue artistic, intellectual, and spiritual ends can do so. Those who wish to pursue materialistic ends can also do so. The only losers are those who wish to impose their values on others.

Let us explore this criticism further by noting that there are (in very general terms) three ways to change people so that they are not so materialistic: one can use persuasion, indoctrination, or coercion. Persuasion is the only alternative that is compatible with a free society. When you try to persuade someone, you present *reasons* for adopting your point of view. Indoctrination involves the presentation and/or reinforcement of *one* point of view in a manner judged most likely to lead to its adoption. Success, not truth, is the main concern. If lies are more likely to be convincing, then lies will be used. If it is helpful to repress opposing views, then opposing views will be repressed. While indoctrination tries to instill the desired beliefs, coercion (the use of force or the threat of force) is used to control people's behavior. Are people too competitive and self-centered? Then the persons who perform actions that exhibit these undesirable qualities will be punished. The persons who decide what qualities are undesirable are assuming that their ends are superior to the ends of the persons they wish to control. They do not grant others an equal right to be free.

In *Anarchy, State, and Utopia,* Nozick presents the following list of persons:

Wittgenstein, Elizabeth Taylor, Bertrand Russell, Thomas Merton, Yogi Berra, Allen Ginsburg, Harry Wolfson, Thoreau, Casey Stengel, The Lubavitcher Rebbe, Picasso, Moses, Einstein, Hugh Hefner, Socrates, Henry Ford, Lenny Bruce, Baba Ram Dass, Ghandi, Sir Edmund Hillary, Raymond Lubitz, Buddha, Frank Sinatra, Columbus, Freud, Norman Mailer, Ayn Rand, Baron Rothschild, Ted Williams, Thomas Edison, H.L. Mencken, Thomas Jefferson, Ralph Ellison, Bobby Fischer, Emma Goldman, Peter Kropotkin, you, and your parents.[11]

This list provides a dramatic illustration of the fact that persons are different. Each person has unique capacities and needs that only he or she can assess. Thus, the development of one's capacities and the satisfaction of one's needs requires freedom from control by others. A free society also allows for freedom of association; persons can join with others in communities that seem attractive to them. If an individual believes that most persons are too materialistic, then he can choose to associate with persons who have nonmaterialistic values. A free society allows for the unique development of each individual. It is utopia.

6.5   Let us take a final look at the welfare problem. Can a society that lacks a comprehensive government program to help the poor be the best possible society? To answer this question, it is helpful to consider what a good welfare program would be like.

I assume that a good welfare program would give aid only to those who are needy. This principle would seem to follow from the very purpose of a welfare system—its purpose is to help the needy. Furthermore, most persons would acknowledge that it is unfair to use taxpayers' money to help persons who are not in need. For example, suppose that I quit my job and demand that taxpayers support me. Taxpayers could rightfully complain that, since I am quite capable of supporting myself, I have no right to demand that others take care of my needs.

A good welfare program should provide assistance that is sufficient for the needy to lead a decent life. This principle is obviously vague, and there is probably no way to make it very exact. What counts as a "decent life" will vary with different times and different cultures. Reasonable persons can disagree about these matters, but extremes can be recognized. For example, an income of $3000 for an urban family of four in the United States in 1981 is too low.

A good welfare program should not remove incentives to work. There are at least two reasons for accepting this principle. First, if a welfare program removes work incentives, persons who could support themselves will stay on the welfare roles which is an unfair burden on taxpayers. Secondly, welfare recipients are seriously harmed by a system that removes work incentives. A class of dependent persons is created who have no incentive to assume responsibility for their own lives.

A good welfare program should be affordable. By this I mean that it should not be so costly that serious damage is done to the overall economy. A welfare system that is too costly will kill the goose that lays the golden eggs. Only affluent societies can afford welfare systems that provide recipients with a decent standard of living. In a poor country like India, serious attempts to "share the wealth" would simply result in universal poverty.

To summarize, I claim that a good welfare system should satisfy (at least) the following principles:

(1) Help should be given only to the needy.
(2) Assistance should be sufficient for the needy to lead a decent life.
(3) Assistance should not remove incentives to work.
(4) The program should be affordable.

If we abolished a welfare system that satisfied these principles, we would certainly lose something of value. However, there is *no* welfare system that can satisfy these principles.

The welfare system presently operating in the United States fails to satisfy (3). In most cases, if a welfare recipient goes to work, he loses benefits. And welfare benefits are often comparable to take-home pay, so the recipient usually has no (financial) incentive to seek employment.[12]

Milton Friedman's "negative income tax" proposal satisfies (3). The following is an example of how his proposal would work:

> In 1978 allowances amounted to $7200 for a family of four, none above age sixty-five. Suppose a negative income tax had been in existence with a subsidy rate of 50 percent of unused allowances. In that case, a family of four that had no income would have qualified for a subsidy of $3600. If members of the family had found jobs

and earned an income, the amount of the subsidy would have gone down, but the family's total income—subsidy plus earnings—would have gone up. If earnings had been $1000, the subsidy would have gone down to $3100 and total income up to $4100.[13]

Under Friedman's proposal, a welfare recipient is always better off financially if he works. But some critics of the proposal claim that it fails to satisfy (2). They would claim, for example, that an income of $3600 is not enough for a family of four to lead a decent life. However, if the income floor is raised to higher level such as $6000, then it becomes doubtful that the proposal satisfies (4). At this level, any family of four with an income less than $12,000 would receive an income subsidy.

Regardless of the level of support, Friedman's proposal violates (1). Persons are guaranteed a certain income whether they are capable of supporting themselves or not. Thus the proposal assumes that we have the right to seize part of the earned income of some persons in order to support other persons who choose not to work. One does not have to be a libertarian to recognize that this is an immoral policy. To Friedman's credit, he does not offer his proposal as a final solution to the welfare problem. He says that his proposal would "ease the transition from where we are to where we would like to be."[14]

What is the libertarian solution to the problem of poverty? Obviously, governmental policies that make it difficult for persons to find employment or to start businesses should be changed. Among other things, minimum wage laws and licensing laws should be abolished, the laws granting special privileges to labor unions should be repealed, and the social security tax (which raises the cost of labor) should be terminated. Looking at the problem of poverty in more general terms, the only good solution is affluence. In the United States, per capita disposable income (in dollars adjusted for inflation) rose by 112 percent between 1939 and 1969.[15] If real per capita income were to double in the next thirty years, there would be very little poverty in the United States. And those who were in financial distress could be easily helped by family, friends, churches, or private charities.

6.6 There would be no public schools in a libertarian society. Would this be a serious loss? Let us begin to answer this question by noting that public schools in the United States have serious problems. Vandalism, violence, and theft are quite common.[16] The increase in disciplinary problems has been coupled with a serious decline in students' scores on national tests.[17] And while the performance of students has worsened, expenditures on public education have increased. Since 1960, per pupil expenditures (in inflation adjusted dollars) have more than doubled.[18]

Many Americans are disturbed by the fact that the problems of public schools have not responded to the traditional governmental remedy (spending more money). Americans like to think that all problems are solvable. However, tinkering with the system will not cure the sickness of public education, for the sickness is due to the very nature of the system. Public schools do not have to provide good service because they have a captive clientele. The government requires that children go to school, and parents are compelled to pay taxes to support the public school system. Most parents are unwilling or unable to pay taxes and pay tuition to send their children to private schools. Hence, public schools get students regardless of their performance. In contrast, if all schools were private (as they would be in a libertarian society), they would have to provide good service or they would not attract students. The existence of a private school depends on its ability to satisfy its customers.

The bureaucratic nature of the public school system is another cause of the poor performance of public schools. At best, bureaucracies provide mediocre and impersonal service. Bureaucracies are noted for their red tape and for the deadening uniformity of their rules and regulations. Innovation is frowned upon, and changes must be approved by the bureaucratic hierarchy. The bureaucratic rules are supposed to benefit the "average student," but there is no average student. Each student has unique abilities, aptitudes, interests, and aspirations. What is needed is far greater diversity in education. We need a variety of schools with diverse programs that will serve the needs of different students. In contrast to bureaucracies, markets are noted for their diverse products and services. For example, consider the wide variety of publications in the United States. If your particular interests happen to be rock collecting, sky diving, astrology, and socialism, you can find books and magazines that cater to your interests. Would the publishing industry be as diverse if it were controlled by the government? Very unlikely! A free market in education would produce far greater diversity, and as a result, parents, students, and teachers would all be better served.

The compulsory nature of the public school system is another reason for its poor performance. Many students do not want to go to school and, as a result, they rebel. And as every teacher knows, two or three troublemakers in a class can make teaching virtually impossible. The wide variety of schools that would develop in a free educational market could help to solve this problem. However, there would still be children who do not have the aptitude or the interest to benefit from further schooling. There is no good reason to compel these children to go to school.

To sum up, far from being a serious loss, the abolition of public schools would breathe new life into our educational system. A free market in education would produce the diversity in educational opportunities that is so sorely needed. Parents would take a greater interest in their children's education, for they would actually have some control over the instruction their children receive. Students would be able to go to schools that are far more responsive to their individual needs. And teachers could use their creative talents to introduce students to the joys of learning.

6.7 In *The Republic,* Plato describes his utopian society. He then goes on to speculate about how this society, if it were established, would eventually degenerate.

> Hard as it may be for a state so framed to be shaken, yet, since all that comes into being must decay, even a fabric like this will not endure forever, but will suffer dissolution.[19]

Plato provides us with a sobering reminder of the frailty of human institutions. Thus, it behooves us to consider how the dangers to a free society can be minimized.

The abuse of power by government is an obvious concern. In a free society, political officials would be elected or appointed by elected officials, (5.7). This provides a check on their possible abuse of power; those politicians who misbehave can be removed from their offices. Still, a majority of citizens might favor immoral policies. This introduces the vexatious problem that so concerned James Madison—the problem of the tyranny of the majority. Libertarians believe that persons have rights which should not be taken away by the political process. Freedom of religion, for example, should not be subject to a vote. As we have noted, one way to protect important rights is to stipulate in a constitution that certain rights are "above politics." This procedure can be implemented by the process of judicial review wherein legislation that violates the constitution is nullified.[20]

The "tyranny of minorities" has proven to be as serious a problem for democracies as the tyranny of the majority. Many minority groups have special interests for which they lobby. For example, members of the textile industry want protective tariffs. Such tariffs would be harmful to the majority of citizens (6.2), but most citizens are relatively apathetic about this issue. In contrast, the affected special interest group cares very much about this legislation; their efforts at getting special favors are usually well organized and well financed. The politicians who support their position can usually trade votes with other politicians who wish to pass their own special interest legislation. When the vote-trading is completed, the public is often the loser. In the United States, the President can veto special interest legislation. The President is the only political official who is elected by voters in all the States, and he can claim a mandate to look after the "larger" interests of the country. Judicial vetoes of special interest legislation would also help. Protective tariffs, for example, violate the right of individuals to participate in voluntary economic exchanges. If such a right were guaranteed by the Constitution, the courts could nullify this type of legislation.

We have seen that the separation of powers (legislative, executive, and judicial) can provide a check on the abuse of power by politicians. However, no system of government can provide a guarantee that political officials will not abuse their powers. The ultimate check on politicians must lie with the citizens. Civil disobedience, the refusal to obey, can nullify immoral laws and policies. For instance, suppose the government declares that an "emergency" exists, and thus it is necessary to reinstitute the income tax and the military draft. Non-cooperation is the surest way to stop these policies. If enough citizens refuse to surrender their freedoms, the government cannot take them away.

6.8 The government can do serious damage to a free society by inflating its currency. Henry Hazlitt provides us with a succinct summary of some of the evils of inflation.

> Inflation, to sum up, is the increase in the volume of money and bank credit in relation to the volume of goods. It is harmful

because it depreciates the value of the monetary unit, raises everybody's cost of living, imposes what is in effect a tax on the poorest (without exemptions) at as high a rate as the tax on the richest, wipes out the value of past savings, discourages future savings, redistributes wealth and income wantonly, encourages and rewards speculation and gambling at the expense of thrift and work, undermines confidence in the justice of a free enterprise system, and corrupts public and private morals.[21]

It is important to note that these evils are not offset by long-term gains in production. In fact, inflation leads eventually to lower productivity for two main reasons. First, it creates uncertainty. During an inflationary period, the prices of goods and services do not rise at a uniform rate: the prices of some things rise quickly, some prices rise slowly or not at all, and the price of other things may even drop. This diversity in price changes is masked when the government reports the "average inflation rate." While some producers make high profits during inflationary periods, it is difficult for any particular producer to know what his future profits (if any) will be. Furthermore, inflation makes it difficult for businessmen to determine what their present profits are. The value of their inventories may increase, but how much will it cost to replace them? Businessmen will also question whether they are taking adequate depreciation on their plants and equipment, for they cannot be certain what the replacement costs will be. During an inflationary period, businesses often report profits when they are really using up their capital. Finally, businessmen will be concerned about what action the government may take to control inflation. Will there be a recession or depression? These uncertainties lead eventually to a reluctance on the part of the business community to make new investments.

A second reason why inflation causes lower productivity (in the long run) is that a "cheap money" policy encourages bad investments. When the government starts the process of inflating the currency, interest rates drop. This creates an artificial stimulus for business investment, and the increase in the money supply creates an artificial demand for goods like certain luxury items.

Because inflation leads inevitably to distortions in the interest rate, because during it nobody knows what future prices, costs, or price-cost relations are likely to be, it inevitably distorts and unbalances the structure of production. It gives rise to multitudinous illusions. Because the nominal interest rate, though it rises, does not rise enough, funds are more heavily borrowed than before, uneconomic ventures are encouraged; corporations making high nominal profits invests abnormal sums in expansion of plant. Many regard this, when it is happening, as a happy byproduct of inflation. But when the inflation is over much of this investment is found to have been misdirected—to have been malinvestment, sheer waste. And when the inflation is over, also, there is found to be, because of this previous misdirection of investment, a real and sometimes intense capital shortage.[22]

The artificial "boom" created by cheap money leads inevitably to recession or depression.

Not only is the policy of inflating the currency bad economics; it is a moral disaster as well. Persons who have worked hard in order to save money for future investments or for their retirement years find that the value of their savings have been arbitrarily depreciated. In the United States, a dollar saved in 1940 is now worth less than twenty cents. Furthermore, by inflating the currency, the government is pursuing the dishonest policy of repaying its debts with cheap money. Adam Smith saw through this ruse long ago.

When national debts have once been accumulated to a certain degree, there is scarce, I believe, a single instance of their having been fairly and completely paid. The liberation of the public revenue, if it has ever been brought about at all, has always been brought about by a bankruptcy; sometimes by an avowed one, but always by a real one, though frequently by a pretended payment....

The honor of a state is surely very poorly provided for, when, in order to cover the disgrace of a real bankruptcy, it has recourse to a juggling trick of this kind, so easily seen through, and at the same time so extremely pernicious.[23]

Something should also be said about the morality of governments incurring budget deficits as a normal operating procedure. Suppose that Peter borrows money from Paul, and Peter promises that John will repay the debt. However, Peter has not received permission from John to make this promise. This is analogous to what politicians do when they continuously vote for deficit spending. Since future generations have not given their consent, the politicians have no right to saddle them with this burden.

The obvious solution to the inflation problem is for the government to stop inflating the currency. Instead, a stable monetary framework should be established that will allow the free market to operate efficiently.[24] Unfortunately this cure cannot be painless. The bad investments caused by cheap money must be liquidated, and this will result in economic dislocation.

Chapter Seven

Why Be Moral?

7.1 Persons *ought* to do what is morally right and refrain from doing what is morally wrong. The moral "ought" is categorical which means that it is final or overriding. If acting morally conflicts with doing other good things, one should choose to act morally. The categorical nature of morality can be expressed by saying that we have a *duty* to do what is morally right. The morally good person does his duty voluntarily. It is not the fear of punishment, for example, that motivates him to act morally. The morally good person pays his debts, refrains from stealing, takes care of his children, etc. because he recognizes that these acts are right. He may have other motives as well (e.g., he loves his children), but the desire to do his duty would be (by itself) a sufficient motive.

Moral goodness is a virtue. I understand a virtue to be a quality that contributes to good character. Other examples are compassion, generosity, self-discipline, and fortitude. The compassionate person has a disposition to help others when they are in need. The generous person has a disposition to share his good fortune with others even though they are not in need. For example, the generous person may give a gift to a friend even though the friend could easily buy the item himself. We know that compassion and generosity are good because we value the experience when we are the recipients of compassionate and generous acts. And if compassionate and generous acts are good when we are recipients, consistency requires that we acknowledge that they are good when we are agents as well.

The person with self-discipline can control the impulse to seek immediate gratification when, according to his own values, this impulse conflicts with more important long-range desires. I understand fortitude to be a combination of courage and determination. The person with fortitude is not easily deterred from the pursuit of his important ends. When obstacles and difficulties arise, he does not give up unless they make it impossible for him to achieve the goals he has set for himself. We know that self-control and fortitude are good because the person who lacks these qualities will often regret his previous actions. He will fail to pursue his most important ends, and thus he will not achieve his most valuable goals.

Since moral judgments are categorical, moral goodness is the most important virtue. Why is this so? The importance of acting morally can be seen by considering what life would be like if it were normal for persons to act immorally. In a world in which immoral acts were the norm, no one could be trusted. Lying, stealing, and cheating would be common, and disputes would often be settled by violence. To borrow a famous phrase from Hobbes, life in such a world would be "solitary, poor, nasty, brutish, and short."[1] Human beings need the cooperation of others, and social cooperation would be impossible if most persons acted immorally. Thus, the necessity for social cooperation is the "raison d'etre" of morality.

An egoist might reply that this argument gives him a good reason for holding that *others* ought to be moral. However, *he* has no reason to be moral. In reply, if the egoist grants that others ought to be moral, consistency requires him to acknowledge that he ought to be moral as well. He can (logically) claim an exemption only if he is relevantly different. But he is not relevantly different. The egoist, like other persons, needs the cooperation of others.

According to the moral theory that I have developed, a person's basic duty is to grant other persons an equal right to be free. In most cases, we fulfill this duty by leaving others alone, i.e., by refraining from interfering with their activities. Many persons will feel that this conception of morality is too narrow. Isn't compassion, for example, a moral virtue? While compassion is certainly a virtue, it is not a *moral* virtue. Acting morally is more than a good or nice thing to do. It is our duty to do what is right, and thus acting morally is a requirement that we cannot evade by deciding that there are other good things to do instead. Because moral judgements are categorical, the content of morality is supplied by our various duties. And according to the freedom principle, a person does not have a duty to help others unless he voluntarily accepts or creates such a duty, (1.4). Thus, compassionate acts exceed the requirements of morality.

I am using the words 'duty' and 'right' in the strict sense in which duties entail correlative rights and rights entail correlative duties. In recent times, we have seen a proliferation of right-claims. It has been claimed that persons have the right to a job, the right to periodic holidays with pay, the right to share in the benefits of scientific advancement, etc.[2] Due to this inflation of right-claims, the moral currency has been cheapened. The concept of a right has become an ill-defined and hazy notion which persons use to press their demands for whatever they would like to have. If the notion of a right is to regain its value, we must resist the loose talk about rights. Since persons ought to grant others their rights, rights are (in principle) enforceable. Thus, when a person claims the right to something, we should insist that he tell us who (what individual or group) has the duty to grant him this right. When the strict notion of a right is combined with acceptance of the freedom principle, we see that many right-claims are illegitimate. For example, a person may have a right to a vacation with pay because this right is in his employment contract. But persons in general do not have this right; there are no individuals or groups who can be justifiably coerced in order to compel them to grant all persons this "right." In conclusion, if persons have as their basic right the equal right to be free, general right-claims to things like a job and vacations with pay are spurious.

7.2 Let us review the argument for adopting the moral point of view. We have noted that the importance of acting morally can be seen by imagining what life would be like if it were normal for persons to violate the rights of others. If acting immorally were the norm, all trust would vanish and social cooperation would be impossible. However, man is a social animal; we need the cooperation of others. Thus we see the *necessity* for adopting the moral point of view. Since morality is a necessity, moral judgments are final or overriding; they specify what, all things considered, we ought to do.

Since each of us needs the cooperation of others, we have an obvious reason for holding that *others* ought to be moral. Furthermore, once it is acknowledged that others ought to act morally, consistency requires that each person grant that he should be moral also. If I believe, for example, that others ought to pay their debts, keep their promises, refrain from stealing, etc., then I must acknowledge that I should do the same.

When one adopts the moral point of view, one accepts the idea that acting morally is more important than doing other good things. Suppose that an artist is contemplating abandoning his wife and children in order to make it easier for him to pursue his career. Let us assume that the artist admits that it would be immoral for him to leave his wife and children. Still he asks "Why should I be moral?" I would answer the artist's question by presenting the argument for adopting the moral point of view. Assuming that the artist finds the argument to be persuasive, he will have the answer to his question. He ought to do what is morally right because in doing so he is doing what, according to his own beliefs, is most valuable.

This answer to the question "Why be moral?" is often overlooked because of the common assumption that there is a conflict between morality and self-interest.[3] For example, suppose that Jones could get away with not repaying a debt, i.e., any sanctions brought against him would be less burdensome than the benefit derived from keeping the money. It is often assumed that it would be in Jones's self-interest not to repay the debt. But why should we make this assumption? What *really* is in a person's interest? We cannot know what is in a person's interest without taking account of what it is that the person values. It is safe to assume that Jones does value keeping his money. But suppose he believes that acting morally is more valuable than keeping his money. In this case, it would be in his self-interest to repay the debt. In general, it is in a person's interest to live a good life. (Surely it is not in one's self-interest to live a bad life.) A person lives the best possible life, according to his own values, when he does what is most valuable. And if one believes that acting morally is more valuable than doing other good things, then acting morally is in one's self-interest.

Persons who act contrary to their own moral beliefs often experience guilt and shame. They feel shame because they have let others down. They feel guilt because they have let themselves down; they have not lived up to their own values. The desire to avoid feelings of guilt and shame plays a role in motivating persons to act morally. However, such feelings are *not* reasons for acting morally. One must first have the relevant beliefs about what is moral and immoral before he will feel guilt or shame. These beliefs can often be instilled by indoctrination and conditioning. Correct moral beliefs can also be acquired by understanding the reasons for accepting the freedom principle along with the principle's implications. And once one has acquired the correct moral beliefs, feelings of guilt and shame can play their role in motivating moral behavior.[4]

The moral philosopher presents arguments in order to persuade others to adopt what he considers to be correct moral beliefs. In doing so, he must make two assumptions about other persons: (1) their beliefs about what is right and wrong are amenable to rational persuasion, and (2) what they believe will affect how they act. These assumptions underlie any attempt at deliberation about what is morally right or wrong. When they do not hold, there is no (practical) point to the deliberation. When reason fails to persuade, one can resort to the sanctions of blame and punishment. However, there are steps we can take which could increase the likelihood that individuals will be amenable to rational persuasion. This brings us to the topic of moral education.

7.3 My conception of moral education has been influenced by Lawrence Kohlberg's theory of moral development. Kohlberg claims that there are six stages of moral development. At the highest stages, individuals make moral decisions according to self-chosen moral principles.

It is also evident that moral development in terms of these stages is a progressive movement toward basing moral judgment on concepts of justice. To base a moral duty on a concept of justice is to base that duty on the right of an individual; to judge an act wrong is to judge it as violating such a right. The concept of a right implies a legitimate expectancy, a claim which I may expect others to agree I have. While rights may be grounded on sheer custom or law, there are two general grounds for a right—equality and reciprocity (including exchange, contract, and the reward of merit). At stages 5 and 6 all the demands of statute or moral (natural) law are grounded on concepts of justice, i.e., on agreement, contract, and the impartiality of the law and its function in maintaining the rights of individuals.[5]

The mature moral agent adopts a conception of justice based on equality and reciprocity. He conforms to this conception in order to live up to his own values; his motive for behaving morally is to avoid self-condemnation. Kohlberg believes that there is a natural tendency on the part of most individuals to develop into mature moral agents. However, many persons become "fixated" at a lower stage of development. Hence, the goal of moral education should be to help persons become mature moral agents. As I shall show, this conception of moral education can avoid the problem of moral indoctrination.[6]

The crucial first step in moral education is to overcome the egocentric point of view. Young children are naive egoists; their main concern is to satisfy their own immediate desires. To move beyond this level, two cognitive incapacities must be overcome: lack of imagination and lack of consistency in one's thinking. Advancement can be encouraged by the use of what I shall call golden rule arguments. For example, suppose you are having a discussion with a child about the morality of stealing. You ask the child "Would you think it right for someone to steal one of your toys?" Let us assume that the child says "no." Then you ask whether he thinks it is right for him to steal someone else's toy. There is an obvious appeal to consistency with the point being that the child should make the same judgment when he is the agent or the recipient.

Imagination can also be stimulated by golden rule arguments. You ask the child "How do you feel when someone steals one of your toys?" Let us assume that the child replies that he feels bad. Then you ask "How do you think Johnny feels when you steal one of his toys?" The point of this exercise is to increase the child's capacity for empathy by getting him to imagine how his actions are perceived from the point of view of his recipients.

I would not teach the Golden Rule itself, for it is not a satisfactory moral principle. Its inadequacy can be seen by examining two different formulations. There is the "would want" formulation—Do unto others as you would want them to do unto you. One problem with this formulation is that what you would want if you were the recipient of the proposed action may be quite different from what your actual recipient wants. It might appear that this problem can be handled by stipulating that you should imagine that you have the desires of your recipient. However, this would mean that the judge, for example, should not sentence the criminal because the criminal does not want to go to prison. If a person of questionable integrity asks you for a loan, you should give it to him, etc. This interpretation of the Golden Rule requires perfect altruism; you should always do what others want you to do. Another problem is that this interpretation does not tell us what to do when our acts affect more than one person and our recipients have conflicting desires. For example, the convicted criminal wants to be released, but his victim wants the criminal to be punished. What should the judge do?

One might think that the "would have" formulation of the Golden Rule (i.e., Do unto others as you would *have* them do unto you) avoids some of these problems. However, if it does, it is because it trades on the vagueness and/or ambiguity of the phrase 'would have.' What does 'would have' mean? Let us assume that it does not mean "would want." What other possibilities are there? It could refer to what you think is right. In other words, you should treat others in ways that you would think right if you were the recipient. On this interpretation, the Golden Rule simply calls for consistency. It does not tell us what is right. It assumes that we know what is right, and it exhorts us to be consistent in applying our moral standards—whatever they may be.

This criticism shows the limitations of golden rule arguments. Consistency provides no guarantee that our judgments are correct; we can be consistently wrong as well as consistently right. For example, suppose that you have engaged a child in a discussion of the morality of cheating. You get the child to make inconsistent judgments. He says that it is right for him to cheat but not right for other students to cheat. He may realize that consistency requires him to give up one of the judgments, so, after some reflection, he decides that it must be right for other students to cheat as well. But this, of course, is not the result that you were seeking.

Golden rule arguments can play the important role of increasing the capacity of children to reason about moral issues. However, moral education should move beyond simple appeals to consistency and empathy.[7] I shall call the next stage in moral education "philosophical analysis." The objective of philosophical analysis is to help individuals acquire two more cognitive skills: the ability to recognize underlying values and to determine their implications. This objective is pursued by examining real and imaginary cases in which persons make moral judgments. For example, suppose that a scientist announces that his research demonstrates that smoking marijuana causes a decrease in the smoker's white blood cell count, and, as a result, smokers have a lower resistance to viral infections. On the basis of this information, the scientist concludes that smoking marijuana should be prohibited. What values underlie this normative judgment? Presumably the scientist is assuming that paternalism is justified (at least in this kind of case). Now that we have spotted an underlying value, we can examine its implications. For example, suppose that the scientist determines that smoking cigarettes causes a decrease in the smoker's white blood cell count. Consistency would require that he advocate the prohibition of smoking. Or suppose that we know cigarette smoking increases the smoker's chances of getting lung cancer. Since becoming ill with cancer is more serious than acquiring a viral infection, consistency would again require a ban on cigarette smoking. The point of this kind of exercise is to help persons become aware of the implications of their value assumptions.

At this level of moral education, it is important to examine positions on controversial issues. Many persons become fixated at the stage of authoritarian morality; they uncritically accept the moral views of persons whom they believe are authorities. The examination of controversial issues can stimulate persons to move beyond this stage. It is difficult to believe that the authorities are always right when they disagree with each other. Another strategy is to consider new issues that have not been decided by the so-called authorities. For example, one could examine the moral issues involved in the cloning of human beings. When a new issue is examined, the need to think for oneself should be apparent.

The objective of moral education is to help persons acquire the cognitive abilities necessary for thinking clearly about moral issues. This will foster the development of mature moral agents. The mature moral agent makes consistent moral judgments. His imagination allows him to understand moral issues from the point of view of other persons, i.e., he has the capacity for empathy. He can spot the values that underlie his moral judgments and determine their implications in other cases. Insofar as moral education encourages persons to acquire these cognitive skills, it avoids the problem of moral indoctrination.

However, the mature moral agent will be inclined to adopt a particular moral point of view. He has moved beyond the stage at which the views of "authorities" are accepted without critical evaluation. He values his own autonomy and does not evade his personal responsibility of deciding for himself what is right and wrong. Since he makes consistent judgments, he will recognize that the autonomy of others is also valuable. As a result, it is likely that he will acknowledge the equal right of other persons to decide for themselves what their own good is and how to pursue it. In other words, it is likely that the mature moral agent will accept the freedom principle.

7.4 The argument for adopting the moral point of view shows us (for example) why it is *usually* wrong to lie. However, there are occasions when this moral rule, like most moral rules, can be justifiably broken. I, of course, maintain that we should use the freedom principle to determine when it is morally permissible to break the common moral rules. In support of this claim, I shall conclude this chapter by reviewing the main reasons for accepting the freedom principle.

Persons are (by stipulative definition) autonomous agents; they are capable of formulating and acting on conceptions of how their lives should be lived. The freedom principle requires reciprocal respect for autonomy. Reciprocal respect for autonomy entails that persons have the *same* right to pursue their own good in their own way. In other words, persons have the equal right to be free. One reason for accepting this view is that persons should not impose their values on others.[8] I do not make this claim because I am skeptical that persons can know what is good. On the contrary, we do have knowledge of values; we know that many different things are good. The world is overflowing with good things to do. There are many rewarding activities and many worthy causes to support. There is so much to do, to see, and to learn. Each person has the time and energy to do only a fraction of the things that are worth doing. Given the superabundance of good things to do, no one is justified in compelling others to conform to his particular set of values. No person can know that his valued activities and his worthy causes are best for other persons.

This brings us to a second reason for accepting the freedom principle. Persons are different. Each person has unique capacities and needs. People differ in terms of their feelings, talents, desires, likes and dislikes, aspirations, etc. There is no "average person," and thus social planners cannot make people happy. The individual is the only one who has direct access to his own unique combination of characteristics. He is the only one who can appreciate his special needs. Thus, persons require freedom from interference in order to live fulfilling lives.

A person gives meaning to his life by choosing to pursue ends that he values. Furthermore, a person must be self-directing for *his* life to be good. If the good things in one's life are the result of interference, one cannot take credit for them. When we deny others the right to be responsible for their lives, we take away their opportunity to give meaning to their lives. Meaning cannot be conferred by others; it must be earned by individuals who choose to live worthy lives.

Another reason for accepting the freedom principle is that persons have a special dignity due to their capacity to be self-directing agents. If one denies this, then he implicitly denies his own human worth. If the autonomy of other persons is not worthy of respect, then this casts doubt on the worth of all human projects. This is the road to cynicism and nihilism. The alternative is to acknowledge that one's own autonomy is valuable and the autonomy of others is valuable as well.

Finally, the free society, the society based on reciprocal respect for autonomy, is the best possible society. It is utopia. The free society is morally right, and it is also the best society in terms of two other important social values—social cooperation and economic productivity. According to the freedom principle, interactions should be based on mutual consent. When persons participate in economic interactions, they do so because they expect to gain from this cooperation. When persons exchange goods and services for their mutual benefit, the result is increased productivity. When the government interferes with free markets, the result is misallocation of capital, labor, and resources. Of course, persons are more than economic beings. They have hedonistic, aesthetic, intellectual, an spiritual concerns as well. The free society allows persons to have different aspirations. It gives all persons, except those who wish to impose their values on others, the opportunity to live fulfilling lives.

Appendix

I have tried to write a book that can be understood by persons with no formal training in philosophy. In pursuit of this end, I have postponed an attempt at a more thorough analysis of autonomy, and I have not dealt with the difficult problem of what should be done when tragedies could be avoided by violating persons' rights. I shall undertake these tasks now.

AUTONOMY

Let us review what has been said so far about autonomy. Persons are autonomous in the sense in which they are capable of formulating and acting on conceptions of how their lives should be lived. Autonomous agents can conceive of future alternatives; they understand that they can pursue different ends and employ different means. They have conceptions of value which can be used in deciding what ends to pursue and what means are appropriate. They can recognize conflicts between different ends and control their behavior in order to pursue those ends considered most valuable.

More needs to be said about values. Value is discovered, not conferred. Persons find in their experience that certain things are valuable. Let us consider some examples that illustrate these general remarks. Suppose that Brown decides to try wine tasting because it is the "in" thing to do. Brown does not (at this point) value wine tasting for its own sake; instead he is using it as a means to social acceptance. But, as Brown participates in the activity, he may become interested in learning about wine. The subtlety of good wines intrigues him. Does the wine have too much acid? Too much tannin? How is the balance? Is the bouquet fruity? How is the body? After learning what characteristics to look for, he begins to appreciate the qualities of good wines. Finally, let us assume that he comes to enjoy the taste of good wines. At this point, Brown appreciates the value of wine tasting, but this value was not conferred. Through involvement in the activity, he discovers that the activity is valuable.

Now Brown must make decisions about how much time and money to invest in this activity. Suppose that he tries sailing and finds it to be more satisfying, and he loses interest in wine tasting. He still believes that wine tasting is valuable, but other activities are more valuable.

To cite another example, suppose that Smith hates Jones. Smith is thinking about circulating a false story which would damage Jones's reputation. Smith has a strong inclination to do this, but he is troubled by its morality. He acknowledges that he would consider it wrong for someone else to circulate a false story about him in a similar situation. As a result, he concludes that he should not slander Jones. He also feels remorse for having the immoral inclination in the first place. In this case, Smith discovers that a course of action which had some initial attraction is not valuable.

To value something is to regard it as desirable. Hence, one always has a motive to pursue (or keep) what one values. On the other hand, persons sometimes desire things that they do not value. For example, in a fit of anger, I may have a strong desire to hit my child even though I know that hitting him is not good. To summarize, if something is good, then it is desirable, but if something is desired, it does not follow that it is good. Thus, there may be no value, or even disvalue, in satisfying one's desires.

I do not claim that the autonomous agent always does what he most values. Instead, the autonomous agent is *capable* of acting in accordance with his values. Consider the example of the overweight person who believes that he should get more exercise. However, exercising is painful and the benefits are distant, and thus he does not make the effort. This person could choose to exercise by overruling his present inclination in favor of a future value. He is autonomous, for he is capable of doing what he most values.

The autonomous agent chooses to act on some of his desires, and not to act on others. Even so-called basic drives like hunger and sex do not necessitate particular actions. Suppose that Joe is a hungry vegetarian, but the only food available is a hamburger. Joe desires to eat, but he chooses not to eat the hamburger. Or suppose that Sue has a desire to seduce the attractive executive in the next office. But she decides that it would be immoral to cheat on her husband, so she decides not to act on her desire.

Determinists deny that a person can behave differently than he actually does behave. They claim that choices are necessitated by previous causes. Furthermore, the chain of causes and effects can be traced to factors beyond the agent's control, and thus the belief that persons are (usually) responsible for their choices is an illusion. There are a number of problems with the determinist's thesis. Let us first note that the determinist is using a special conception of causation. In ordinary discourse, we often talk about causes that are neither necessary nor sufficient conditions for the occurrence of events, (1.3). For example, we can say that the fire was caused by a discarded cigarette or that cigarette smoking causes lung cancer. If causes necessitate events, as the determinist maintains, then the word 'cause' must refer to the sufficient conditions for the occurrence of events.

At this point, it becomes clear that the determinist is not offering a thesis that has been proven empirically. We simply do not know the causes (i.e., the sufficient conditions) of much of human behavior. What, for example, caused me to write the last sentence? The determinist is *assuming* that every human behavior has causes which necessitate it; therefore the determinist's belief in determinism is a metaphysical article of faith.

The determinist asks us to give up the belief that persons are (usually) responsible for their choices. This would entail a radical change in our thinking about morality and punishment. But why should we accept this radical change? Surely it is up to the determinist to prove that his thesis is true. However, the determinist lacks the empirical evidence that would prove his point. Furthermore, it is difficult to understand what the determinist could mean if he claimed that he could prove that his thesis is true. If human behavior is determined, then the determinist's claim that determinism is true is necessitated by antecedent causes. If the causes had been different, apparently the determinist could have been determined to claim that determinism is false. On the other hand, if a person's beliefs about determinism (for or against) are not determined by antecedent causes, then the thesis is false. This paradox should (at least) make us skeptical about determinism.

Since serious mistakes are often made due to the failure to make distinctions by using words precisely, I shall conclude this section with a review of some of the relevant terminology. I have stipulated that a person is free to the extent that he is able to pursue his ends without interference. A person is interfered with when others cause him to behave involuntarily by means of force, threat, or deception. The concept of behavior is the genus that includes the class of actions. When a person acts he controls his behavior with the objective of achieving some end. Actions are (by definition) purposive; however, intentional behavior may not be voluntary. I intentionally hand my wallet to the gunman, but I do not give it up voluntarily. An act is involuntary when the agent would not have chosen to perform the act had he not been threatened or ignorant of some relevant fact. The person who tries to cross the bridge that will not hold his weight walks on the bridge intentionally. But this action is involuntary, for he would not have chosen to walk on the bridge had he known that it would collapse. When he falls into the water, his behavior is not intentional, i.e., he is no longer acting. At this point, his behavior is involuntary due to the force of gravity.

Finally, we should distinguish between autonomy, integrity, and authenticity. The autonomous agent has the capacity to act in accordance with his values, but he may choose not to do so. A person has integrity insofar as he does act in accordance with his values. The authentic person does not accept his values secondhand; he does not assume that something is good because the "right people" say so. Instead, he acquires his values through his own personal experience and reflection. While autonomy is an extremely valuable characteristic, persons simply are autonomous, and thus they deserve no credit for having this characteristic. Integrity and authenticity, in contrast, are virtues (qualities that contribute to good character).

TRAGEDY AND RIGHTS

A favorite kind of case for critics of moral theories is the kind in which bad consequences are unavoidable. For example, suppose that two survivors of a shipwreck are struggling to hold onto a plank that will only support one person. If this kind of case is the appropriate test for moral theories, then all theories fail the test. When a tragic outcome is unavoidable, no theory can provide a happy solution. This is not the kind of case that I shall be concerned with in this section. What I shall examine is the kind of case in which tragedy is avoidable—but only at the cost of violating someone's rights.

Suppose that I am fishing and I find another fisherman who is seriously injured. To save his life, it is imperative that I get him to a hospital as quickly as possible, so I hoist him onto my shoulder and begin to walk to my car. The fastest route requires crossing a farmer's field which has a large no trespassing sign. I ignore the sign and start across the field. The farmer appears and complains that I am damaging his corn, and he demands that I walk around his property. I ignore this demand and carry my burden straight to the car. In doing so, I violate the farmer's right to determine who can use his property.

The freedom principle seems to yield a counter-intuitive judgement in this case. I have no duty to help the fisherman, but I do have a duty to respect the farmer's property right. Hence, it is wrong for me to trudge across his field. A possible defense of the freedom principle can be mounted by questioning whether our moral intuitions are trustworthy in a case of this sort. Let us compare our intuitions in this case with another case. Suppose that persons are starving in Cambodia. I send what little money I can to CARE, but not enough money is being sent. I have a rich, miserly uncle who never contributes to charities, and I know where he keeps his spending money and other valuables. Suppose that I break into his house, take money and goods that net me $1000, and I send the $1000 to CARE. As a result, the lives of ten Cambodians are saved. The consensus among my students has been that I should not steal from my uncle. On the other hand, my students have held that I should cross the farmer's field. But it is hard to see why the right-violation is justified in one case and not the other. Admittedly my uncle suffers a more serious loss, but more lives are saved. Perhaps we should conclude that "our moral intuitions" are not very trustworthy.

Still I find the farmer case to the troubling, for I must admit that if I were in that situation I would cross the farmer's field. However, one thing to note is that the case is hypothetical. Furthermore, it assumes that the farmer is extraordinarily callous and insensitive. If real people are not like that, and I have yet to find one in my experience, then this case does not pose a serious problem. If the freedom principle yields counter-intuitive judgments in a few extraordinary cases, this is not a good reason to reject the principle. Every moral theory will have its problem cases, and as Aristotle pointed out, the wise man is satisfied with as high a degree of certainty as the subject matter admits.[1]

Some critics claim that libertarian theories have more than their proper allotment of problem cases. For the most part, they charge that these theories are insensitive to the plight of the poor. I have already argued that poor persons would be better off in a libertarian society. Their basic needs would be met, and they would have the opportunity to improve their financial situation. Admittedly, critics can produce hypothetical cases which seem to be troublesome. I would reply to some of these hypothetical cases by arguing that they do not correspond to the real world. Some cases assume, for example, that most persons are so selfish that they would never lift a hand to help another person unless compelled to do so. If this were true, no moral theory could hope for much success.

Other hypothetical cases are irrelevant because they do not deal with a libertarian society. In a criticism of Nozick's theory, James Fishkin offers the following case dealing with a country that contains an Asian minority group.

> Suppose that the Asians are not the richest, but rather, the poorest minority. And suppose further that there is a temporary food shortage that threatens the poorest sections of the country with starvation. And let us imagine that even though food has been stockpiled for just such an emergency, the government—perhaps realizing that it is only the Asians who would be saved from starvation—does nothing.[2]

Fishkin claims that a libertarian cannot complain if the government does nothing. The appropriate response is that Fishkin's example does not deal with a libertarian society. A libertarian government would have no right to stockpile food for use by some citizens. Where did the government get the authorization and the money to do this?

The problem with many hypothetical cases is that the author fails to specify how the circumstances came about. Events have a history, and the correct account of justice is historical. How, for example, did the poor get to be poor? Furthermore, to answer this kind of question, we must look at individual cases. Social scientists like to talk about the class of poor persons. The members of this "class" will obviously have one thing in common—poverty. But poor persons will be poor for many different reasons. Suppose that Jones is fired from a high paying job because he has sloppy work habits. While he was working, he had plenty of money to buy unemployment insurance, but instead he spent all of his income on riotous living. He cannot find a comparable job because of his past employment record, and he refuses to look for a low paying job because that would be demeaning. As a result, Jones finds himself in a desperate financial situation. Admittedly this is a loaded example. Certainly there will be persons who are poor through no fault of their own. My point is that one must examine individual case histories to find out. And our judgments about whether we should help someone will vary with different histories. A poor person afterall may be needy only in the sense in which he is unwilling (and not unable) to take care of himself.

Fishkin claims that libertarians must be indifferent to helping the needy since "the only value posited is the nonviolation of rights."[3] I do not think that this is a fair criticism of Nozick's theory, and it does not apply to my own views. Helping the needy is good, and thus we should not be indifferent to it. However, since it exceeds the requirements of morality, libertarians will not compel others to be charitable. A libertarian, for example, will not steal from his uncle in order to help the starving Cambodians. What is ultimately at issue in this kind of case is whether one has the right to treat another person "as a mere means" in order to further one's ends. The libertarian says "no." In some cases, this policy can have tragic consequences. However, as Alan Donagan notes, "on any serious view, tragedy is part of human life; and morality goes hand in hand with tragedy."[4]

Notes
Preface

1. If the instructor tolerates cheating, he will (presumably) violate his agreement with his employer.
2. John Locke, *The Second Treatise of Government* (Indianapolis: Bobbs-Merrill, 1952), p. 77.
3. *Ibid.,* p. 124.
4. Henry Thoreau, "Civil Disobedience," *The Portable Thoreau* (New York: Viking Press, 1947), p. 109.

1 The Freedom Principle

1. More will be said about autonomy in Chapter 2 and in the Appendix.
2. The "in most cases" qualification will be examined below.
3. This is a stipulation. In ordinary discourse, the word 'deceive' is usually used only when the agent intends to mislead someone.
4. The word 'freedom' is often given too much work to do, and as a result, it fails to have a clear meaning. To avoid overuse, it is helpful to distinguish between freedom, autonomy, integrity, and authenticity, (see the Appendix).
5. My analysis of the word 'cause' has been influenced by H.L.A. Hart and A.M. Honore, *Causation in the Law* (Oxford: Oxford University Press, 1959).
6. When I use the phrase 'a person's behavior' I am referring to the person's bodily movements or lack of bodily movements. Lying still, for example, is a kind of behavior. When a person acts, he controls his behavior with the objective of achieving some end. Again, an action may involve lack of movement. For example, the person who stands motionless in order to avoid detection is acting.

119

7. My thinking on this topic has been influenced by H.J. McCloskey's article "A Right to Equality?" *Canadian Journal of Philosophy* 6, No. 4 (1976): 625-642.

8. My analysis has been influenced by Alan Gewirth's essay "Political Justice" in *Social Justice* edited by R.B. Brandt (Englewood Cliffs, New Jersey: Prentice Hall, 1962), pp. 119-169.

9. John Stuart Mill, *On Liberty* (New York: Appleton-Century-Crofts, 1947), p. 7.

10. While Mill's liberty principle rules out paternalism, the principle does not apply to all human beings. In particular Mill says that it does not apply to children and mentally incompetent adults.

11. *Ibid.,* p. 75.

12. *Ibid.,* p. 79.

13. *Ibid.,* p. 10.

14. *Ibid.,* p. 9.

15. Alan Donagan, *The Theory of Morality* (Chicago: University of Chicago Press, 1977), p. 203.

16. I have borrowed the phrase 'dominant end' from John Rawls, *A Theory of Justice* (Cambridge: Harvard University Press, 1971), pp. 548-560.

17. Jeremy Bentham, *Introduction to the Principles of Morals and Legislation* (New York: Hafner Publishing, 1948), p. 1.

18. John Rawls, *op. cit.,* p. 557.

2   Paternalism

1. My thoughts on this point have been influenced by an unpublished paper on paternalism written by my colleague George Hole.

2. For a useful discussion of the disadvantages of licensure see Chapter 9 in Milton Friedman, *Capitalism and Freedom* (Chicago: University of Chicago Press, 1962). Among other things, Friedman points out that licensure protects the status quo, and thus it may prevent advances in medicine that would result from the use of novel treatments.

3. Alan Donagan, *The Theory of Morality* (Chicago: University of Chicago Press, 1977), p. 171.

4. Murray Rothbard, *For a New Liberty* (New York: MacMillan Publishing Co., 1978), p. 120.

5. Paul Goodman claims that normal children can make up the first seven years of school-work with four to seven months of good teaching. See *Compulsory Mis-Education* (New York: Vintage Books, 1962), p. 32. Goodman's claim may be an exaggeration, but I do not doubt that a normal teenager can learn to read in a relatively short period of time.

3 Punishment

1. The most prominent defender of this view is Karl Menninger. See *The Crime of Punishment* (New York: The Viking Press, 1968).
2. Randy E. Barnett, "Restitution: A New Paradigm of Criminal Justsice," *Ethics* 87, No. 4 (1977): 279-301.
3. I am not denying that an offender may be culpable due to negligence. For example, we may hold the offender who causes an accident responsible for his offense because he failed to take reasonable precautions to avoid causing the accident.
4. I hold that persons should not violate the freedom principle. However, I do not claim that we get a complete theory of justice from the principle, for an act may be unjust even though it does not violate the principle. For example, a punishment that does not violate the principle may be unjust because it is too severe. That an act violates the freedom principle is a sufficient condition for the act to be (morally) wrong, but it is not a necessary condition.
5. Kenneth Kipnis, "Criminal Justice and the Negotiated Plea," *Ethics* 86, No. 2 (1976): 93-106.
6. One possibility would be to have a three judge panel decide criminal cases. A unanimous verdict would be necessary for conviction. If two of the three judges decide that the accused is guilty, the case would go to a higher court.
7. On this definition, many activities that do not appear on the standard lists of victimless crimes would be classified as victimless crimes. For example, practicing medicine without a license is a victimless crime, (2.3). Many economic activities that are presently illegal (e.g., violating import quotas) are victimless crimes.
8. Although the freedom principle clearly entails that prostitution should be legal, difficult questions remain concerning the regulation of prostitution. For example, should public solicitation be allowed? Should there be restrictions on the location of houses?
9. See Edwin Schur's essay "The Case for Abolition" in Edwin M. Schur and Hugo Adam Bedau, *Victimless Crimes* (Englewood Cliffs, New Jersey: Prentice-Hall 1974), pp. 19-27. Schur argues for the abolition of victimless crimes from a consequential point of view.

4 Property

1. Various versions of the labor theory have been attributed to Locke. However, Locke's theory of property rights is more complex than the caricatures of it that one usually finds in libertarian writings. A more sophisticated treatment of Locke's theory can be found in James Grunebaum's article "Two Justifications of Property," *American Philosophical Quarterly* 17, No. 1 (1980): 53-59. See also Karen I. Vaughn,

"John Locke's Theory of Property," *Literature of Liberty* 3, No. 1 (1980): 5-37.

2. Private property can be owned by more than one person (joint ownership). Likewise, property may be leased by more than one person. While lessees, unlike owners, cannot transfer rights on a permanent basis, they may be able to let others use their leased property (depending on the terms of the lease).

3. Grunebaum, *op. cit.,* p. 54.

4. See Ernest Feder, *The Rape of the Peasantry* (Garden City, New York: Doubleday and Company, 1971).

5. Paternalistic interference might be justified in some cases; hence paternalism is a possible exception to this rule.

6. Murray Rothbard makes a similar point in "The Great Ecology Issue: Conservation and the Free Market," *The Individualist* (February 1970): 3.

7. Alan Donagan makes this point in *The Theory of Morality* (Chicago: University of Chicago Press, 1977), p. 96.

8. Garret Hardin, "The Tragedy of the Commons," *Science* 162 (1968): 1243-1248.

9. Samuel Hays, *Conservation and the Gospel of Efficiency* (Cambridge: Harvard University Press, 1959), p. 51.

10. See (1) Murray Rothbard, *For a New Liberty* (New York: MacMillan Publishing Co., 1978), pp. 242-262, (2) Robert Nozick, *Anarchy, State and Utopia* (New York: Basic Books, 1974), pp. 79-81, and (3) John Hospers, *Libertarianism* (Los Angeles: Nash Publishing, 1971), pp. 69-70.

11. David Henderson makes this point in "Energy As Usual," *Libertarian Review* (October 1980): 53.

12. As David Friedman notes, "The only way to completely stop producing pollution is for all of us to drop dead, and even that would create at least a short-run pollution problem." *The Machinery of Freedom* (New York: Harper and Row, 1973), p. 139.

5 Government

1. Since counterfeiting involves deception, the government can prohibit the counterfeiting of its currency. What the government should not do is to prohibit persons from using *other* currencies.

2. My thoughts on this topic have been influenced by Roger Pilon, "Criminal Remedies: Restitution, Punishment, or Both?" *Ethics* 88, No. 4 (1978): 348-357.

3. I have borrowed this suggestion from Tibor Machan, *Human Rights and Human Liberties* (Chicago: Nelson Hall, 1975), p. 271.

4. Milton Friedman, *Capitalism and Freedom* (Chicago: University of Chicago Press, 1962), p. 28.

5. Under Taft-Hartley, a worker can get out of a union and still keep his job

provided he *continues* to pay union dues. Hence, technically speaking, it is not union membership but the payment of dues that is compulsory. This policy fosters union corruption. Even when workers know that their union leaders are corrupt, they must continue to pay union dues.

6. For a useful analysis of the wide variety of possible educational loan programs, see D. Bruce Johnstone, *New Patterns for College Lending* (New York: Columbia University Press, 1972).

7. Robert Nozick, *Anarchy, State, and Utopia* (New York: Basic Books, 1974), pp. 155-164.

8. *Ibid.,* p. 157

9. *The Buffalo Evening News* (February 4, 1980): 27.

10. See John Rawls, *A Theory of Justice* (Cambridge: Harvard University Press, 1971), p. 226.

11. This example was inspired by Nozick's discussion of "innocent shields," *op. cit.,* p. 35.

12. David Friedman, *The Machinery of Freedom* (New York: Harper and Row, 1973), pp. 185-197.

6 Utopia

1. The word 'tendency' indicates that this is the common result; I am not claiming that this happens in every case. In the discussion that follows, I will be drawing a number of general conclusions. Again, these conclusions will not hold in every (particular) case.

2. I am referring to government interference with *voluntary* economic exchanges. Government intervention to prevent pollution, for example, raises different issues, (4.5). Such interference will lower productivity, but the "trade off" (i.e., lower pollution) may be worth it.

3. Henry Hazlitt, *Economics in One Lesson* (New Rochell, New York: Arlington House, 1979), pp. 98-102.

4. Paul Samuelson, *Economics* (New York: McGraw-Hill, 1961), p. 723.

5. For the empirical evidence that minimum wage laws cause unemployment, see Walter E. Williams, *Youth and Minority Unemployment* (Stanford: Hoover Institution Press, 1977), pp. 6-16.

6. Milton Friedman, *Capitalism and Freedom* (Chicago: University of Chicago Press, 1962) p. 123. By 1976, union membership had dropped to about 20 percent of the work force [Robert Flanagan, "American Unions Face 1980," *The Stanford Magazine* 7, No. 1 (1979), p. 39].

7. *Ibid.,* p. 124.

8. I shall say no more about the problems associated with technical monopolies, (see 5.3).

9. Recently there has been some progress toward deregulating the trucking industry.

10. John Hospers, *Libertarianism* (Los Angeles: Nash Publishing, 1971), p. 195.

11. Robert Nozick, *Anarchy, State, and Utopia* (New York: Basic Books, 1974), p. 310.

12. Tom Bethell, "Treating Poverty," *Harper's* (February 1980): 22-24. See also Martin Anderson, *Welfare* (Stanford: Hoover Institution Press, 1978), pp. 43-56.

13. Milton and Rose Friedman, *Free to Choose* (New York: Harcourt Brace Jovanovich, 1979), pp. 121-122.

14. *Ibid.,* p. 119.

15. Henry Hazlitt, *The Conquest of Poverty* (New Rochelle, New York: Arlington House, 1976), p. 43. This calculation is based on data from the Department of Commerce. Real per capita income continued to rise during the 1970's at an average rate of about 3 percent per year until 1978. In 1979 and 1980, real per capita income dropped (*The Wall Street Journal,* December 2, 1980, p. 56). Inflation, high taxes, and increased governmental regulation of the economy have produced serious economic problems. The chickens are coming home to roost.

16. In the 1978-79 school year 110,000 teachers, 5 percent of the U.S. total, reported that they were attacked by students. One in eight high school teachers says that he hesitates to confront students out of fear. One in every four reports that he has had personal property stolen at school. (*Time,* June 16, 1980, p. 59).

17. SAT scores have been declining since 1964 except for 1978 when the average score on the verbal test was roughly equal to the previous year. (*Reason,* September 1979, p. 20).

18. *op. cit., Time,* p. 58.

19. Plato, *The Republic* (New York: Oxford University Press, 1945), pp. 268-269.

20. Since judges are fallible human beings, it is dangerous to give them an absolute veto power. One solution would be to allow the legislature to override a judicial veto by a two-thirds or three-fourths vote.

21. Henry Hazlitt, *The Inflation Crisis and How to Resolve It* (New Rochelle, New York: Arlington House, 1978), p. 41.

22. *Ibid.,* p. 125.

23. Adam Smith, *The Wealth of Nations* (New York: Random House, 1937), pp. 882, 883.

24. In *Capitalism and Freedom* (p. 54), Milton Friedman recommends a "legislative rule" according to which the Federal Reserve Board would be required to increase the money supply at an annual rate between 3 and 5 percent. Critics such as Henry Hazlitt claim that such a rule would become "a political football" because legislators could not resist the temptation to change the rule in order to "fine tune" the economy. In *Free to Choose* (p. 308), Friedman advocates a constitutional amendment that would require a 3 to 5 percent

annual increase in the money supply. If this proposal were implemented, it would provide far more stability than past policies of the Fed. However, there is no guarantee that the economy will grow between 3 and 5 percent a year, and thus the proposal could result in creeping inflation. Creeping inflation is better than galloping inflation, but an inflation rate of only 2 percent a year will erode the purchasing power of the dollar by about half in each generation, (Hazlitt, *op. cit.,* p. 80). All things considered, I think that the best policy is for the government to simply stop inflating the money supply, i.e., keep the money supply stable.

7 Why Be Moral?

1. Thomas Hobbes, *Leviathan* (Indianapolis: Bobbs-Merrill, 1958), p. 107.
2. *Universal Declaration of Human Rights* adopted by the General Assembly of the United Nations (1948).
3. For example, Kurt Baier states that "the very raison d'etre of a morality is to yield reasons which overrule the reasons of self-interest..." *The Moral Point of View* (New York: Random House, 1965), p. 150. Alan Gewirth states that "morality purports to set, for everyone's conduct, requirements that take precedence over all other modes of guiding action, including even the self-interest of the persons to whom it is addressed." *Reason and Morality* (Chicago: University of Chicago Press, 1978), p. 1.
4. Excessive feelings of guilt or shame can be very debilitating. I agree with Peter Breggin that there is only one value to guilt and shame—"their usefulness as signals that the person must become more self-determining and more ethical in his or her thoughts and actions." *The Psychology of Freedom* (Buffalo: Prometheus Books, 1980), p. 110.
5. Lawrence Kohlberg, "Moral Development," *International Encyclopedia of the Social Sciences,* Vol. 10 (1968): 490.
6. My conception of moral education has been *influenced* by Kohlberg's theory. However, there are aspects of his theory that I do not agree with. Also, the following ideas are my own, and the reader should not assume that Kohlberg would agree with them.
7. A more extensive discussion of the limitations of golden rule arguments can be found in my "Formal Moral Arguments," *The Personalist* 53, No. 1 (1972): 25-42.
8. While persons should not impose their values on others, they can defend themselves, (3.1).

Appendix

1. Aristotle, *Ethics* (Baltimore: Penguin Books, 1955), pp. 27-28.

2. James S. Fishkin, *Tyranny and Legitimacy* (Baltimore: Johns Hopkins University Press, 1979), p. 6.
3. *Ibid.,* p. 80.
4. Alan Donagan, *The Theory of Morality* (Chicago: University of Chicago Press, 1977), p. 172.

Selected Bibliography

Anderson, Martin. *Welfare*. Stanford: Hoover Institution Press, 1978.

Aristotle. *Ethics*. Baltimore: Penguin Books, 1955.

Baier, Kurt. *The Moral Point of View*. New York: Random House, 1965.

Becker, Lawrence C. *On Justifying Moral Judgments*. New York: Humanities Press, 1973.

_____. *Property Rights*. London: Routledge and Kegan Paul, 1977.

Dahl, Robert A. *Preface to Democratic Theory*. Chicago: University of Chicago Press, 1956.

Donagan, Alan. *The Theory of Morality*. Chicago: University of Chicago Press, 1977.

Feinberg, Joel. *Rights, Justice, and the Bounds of Liberty.* Princeton: Princeton University Press, 1980.

_____. *Social Philosophy.* Englewood Cliffs, New Jersey: Prentice-Hall, 1973.

Fishkin, James S. *Tyranny and Legitimacy.* Baltimore: Johns Hopkins University Press, 1979.

Friedman, David. *The Machinery of Freedom.* New York: Harper and Row, 1973.

Friedman, Milton. *Capitalism and Freedom.* Chicago: University of Chicago Press, 1962.

Friedman, Milton and Rose. *Free to Choose.* New York: Harcourt Brace Jovanovich, 1979.

George, Henry. *Progress and Poverty.* New York: Robert Schalkenbach Foundation, 1938.

Gewirth, Alan. *Reason and Morality.* Chicago: University of Chicago Press, 1978.

Hare, R.M. *Freedom and Reason.* Oxford: Oxford University Press, 1963.

Hart, H.L.A. *Punishment and Responsibility.* Oxford: Oxford University Press, 1968.

Hart, H.L.A. and Honore, A.M. *Causation in the Law.* Oxford: Oxford University Press, 1959.

Hayek, F.A. *The Constitution of Liberty.* Chicago: University of Chicago Press, 1960.

_____. *The Road to Serfdom.* Chicago: University of Chicago Press, 1944.

Hazlitt, Henry. *The Conquest of Poverty.* New Rochelle, New York: Arlington House, 1973.

_____. *Economics in One Lesson.* New Rochelle, New York: Arlington House, 1979.

_____. *The Inflation Crisis, And How To Resolve It.* New Rochelle, New York: Arlington House, 1978.

Honderich, Ted. *Punishment: The Supposed Justifications.* New York: Harcourt, Brace and World, 1969.

Hospers, John. *Libertarianism.* Los Angeles: Nash Publishing, 1971.

Kant, Immanuel. *Fundamental Principles of the Metaphysic of Morals.* Indianapolis: Bobbs-Merrill, 1949.

Locke, John. *The Second Treatise of Government.* Indianapolis: Bobbs-Merrill, 1952.

Lyons, David. *Forms and Limits of Utilitarianism.* Oxford: Oxford University Press, 1965.

Machan, Tibor. *Human Rights and Human Liberties.* Chicago: Nelson Hall, 1975.

_____. *The Pseudo-Science of B.F. Skinner.* New Rochell, New York: Arlington House, 1974.

Mill, John Stuart. *On Liberty.* New York: Appleton-Century-Crofts, 1947.

Narveson, Jan. *Morality and Utility.* Baltimore: Johns Hopkins Press, 1967.

Norton, David. *Personal Destines.* Princeton: Princeton University Press, 1976.

Nozick, Robert. *Anarchy, State, and Utopia.* New York: Basic Books, 1974.

Rawls, John. *A Theory of Justice.* Cambridge: Harvard University Press, 1971.

Rothbard, Murray. *For A New Liberty.* New York: MacMillan, 1978.

_____. *Power and Market.* Kansas City: Sheed Andrews and McMeel, 1970.

Samuelson, Paul. *Economics.* New York: McGraw-Hill, 1961.

Sartre, Jean-Paul. *Being and Nothingness.* New York: Philosophical Library, 1956.

Singer, Marcus. *Generalization in Ethics.* New York: Alfred A. Knopf, 1961.

Spencer, Herbert. *Social Statistics.* New York: Robert Schalkenbach Foundation, 1970.

Wolff, Robert Paul. *The Autonomy of Reason.* New York: Harper and Row, 1973.